For God's Sake

About the Author

Dr Camillus Metcalfe spent forty years as a nun attached to a convent in the Midlands where she worked as a teacher of German and English. She studied Psychoanalysis and Consultancy to Organisations at the Tavistock Centre in London and lectured for ten years on the MA in Drama Therapy at NUI Maynooth. She worked as a consultant to staff in residential childcare in the HSE and taught the Counselling Skills Certificate Course in NUI Maynooth. Currently she lives near Carrick on Shannon and works part-time as a therapist, supervisor and organisational consultant.

For God's Sake

The Hidden Life of Irish Nuns

Camillus Metcalfe

The Liffey Press

Published by
The Liffey Press Ltd
Raheny Shopping Centre, Second Floor
Raheny, Dublin 5, Ireland
www.theliffeypress.com

A catalogue record of this book is
available from the British Library.

ISBN 978-1-908308-64-1

Cover art from a watercolour original, 'March of the Irish
Nuns', by Liz Hess © 2012 www.lizhess.com

Printed in Ireland by Sprint-Print

Contents

My sincere thanks to the ten women who so willingly shared their life experiences. Their bravery, honesty and courage have opened the door on a story that waited to be told.

'How do I know what I think until I see what I say?'
E.M. Forster

Introduction

The idea for this research began in the late 1990s, as the population in Ireland continued to reel under the shock of revelations of abuse by priests and nuns[1] that daily streamed through television, radio and print media. As a long-standing and dedicated member of a congregation of religious sisters, I found it difficult to maintain a balanced perspective on what was being portrayed.

Before the Second Vatican Council (Vatican II, 1962–65) permitted the opening up of convents – to allow nuns out and the public in – the perception in society was that nuns were holy people who spent their time praying and working. Convents, at this time, existed apart from the world; they were hidden, as was the life within their walls. In this book ten nuns tell the story of their lives in their respective congregations. The older nuns, in their limited contact with family and friends, did not usually speak about their experiences, which makes this research unique in this respect. The stories cover the period 1930 when the first nun, Teresa, entered the convent, until 2008 when the research concluded.

Following the revelations of abuse in the media and an alleged case of abuse by a nun I knew, I began to wonder about the paradoxical nature of religious life. Firstly, there was the perception of nuns as holy, perfect and beyond reproach; women who had publicly vowed, in God's name, to love and care for the poor, and secondly, the reality of wounded and often cruel human beings who had little compassion for those entrusted to their care. I wondered how one could reconcile a life of dedication to the love of God and one's neighbour with acts of cruelty and abuse on that same neighbour. I wondered why no one noticed the abuse and, if they noticed, why it had to be denied. Investigations into institutional abuse began in the late 1990s and it is alleged that a lawyer, engaged in this work, made a link between the oppressive conditions under which the nuns lived and the abuse of those in their care. I began to reflect on this.

My experience of religious life began when the life was already changing and I wondered what it had been like in the past. Most of the nuns with whom I lived and worked were, in spite of their human foibles, decent human beings who were committed to prayer and hard work and looking after those in their care. In everyday life in the convent, praise was always in short supply, while punishment for misdemeanours was unstinting, especially in the earlier period. Many aspects of the life did not make sense, but there was no questioning. Conformity was the order of the day and companionship and humour kept people sane.

Finding a number of nuns prepared to share their stories with another was not an easy task, even for someone who was an insider. Life inside the convent has not often been shared with outsiders, and I am aware that my colleagues were often too ashamed to speak to their families about some of the demands of the life, for fear of being thought ridiculous.

The research was conducted over a period of three years (2005–2008) using a series of three life story interviews. The nuns came from different convents and from three congregations. Eight of them entered the convent between 1930 and 1955. They were teachers, as were most of the religious in Ireland in the mid-twentieth century. All have remained in the convent.

Lily entered in 1972 and worked in an industrial school and also spent a short time working in the Magdalen laundries. Becky entered in 1985. She was a social worker who did not fit into her middle-class teaching order. Both Lily and Becky left the convent after some years. There are no representatives of the lay sisters who did the domestic work in the convent and in the boarding school, and who often worked in the Magdalen laundries and industrial schools.

At the beginning of the first interview I told the nuns the theme of the research, that we would meet three times in all and I invited them to take part. They were free, at this point, not to continue but all ten continued. I explained that, in the first two meetings, I would like them to tell me their stories and that, in the third meeting, I would ask some questions and we would talk together about the issues that arose. The initial meetings gave sufficient time for them to experience a new empathic form of listening and to build enough trust to discuss the issues, without fear or suspicion. Through their engagement with the research, the nuns were reflecting on their lives, perhaps for the first time. This was an opportunity for retrospection and evaluation in a holding environment. Up until now, they had lived their adult lives firstly as a collective, where individual life was discouraged, if not forbidden, and then after Vatican II as individuals trying to redefine and assume their individuality.

Historical research reveals that religious orders played an indispensable part in the functioning of the Irish Church and society since the mid-nineteenth century. The male-dominated, hierarchical Church, while using the sisters for its own purposes, had little real respect for them. These women, on the other hand, benefitted from the prestige and respect of society and thousands flocked to be part of it, all gaining professional status, with some attaining important positions as managers of hospitals or headmistresses in schools – positions that would other-wise have been beyond their reach.[2] The number of nuns in Ire-land grew from 200 in 1800 to 9,000 in 1900 and to 16,000 by the mid-1960s.[3]

The involvement of the religious suited the State because re-ligious labour was cheap or free and the capital costs were met by fundraising from the people and through dowries brought in by the middle class religious.[4] There was little supervision by the State of the institutions run by nuns, especially the industrial schools and the Magdalen Laundries, because there was a belief in the altruism of the nuns and a fear of challenging the Catholic Church. The inmates in these institutions lacked powerful con-nections which isolated them from public scrutiny.[5] The power of the Church/State union was pitted against the powerlessness of those without advocacy. At the same time, inside the convent walls power and powerlessness were juxtaposed.

The teachers and nurses were usually educated and received professional training for their work. Until the 1970s, there was no professional training for the sisters who worked in industrial schools. Those who worked in Magdalen asylums received no professional training. The lay sisters were treated as servants, uneducated and untrained professionally for the work they car-ried out. The system of having lay sisters originated in the Mid-dle Ages when it was customary for wealthy women who entered the cloister to bring their serving women with them, while those who were young were often accompanied by their nurses. There is no evidence that there were lay sisters during the eighteenth century in Ireland, when convents and Catholic schools were for-bidden to function by state law. With the resurgence of religious life for women in the nineteenth century, the lay sister became a visible structure within the convent. The practice of having lay sisters has existed in apostolic congregations until Vatican II (1962–65) called for an end to discrimination in convents.[6]

There was a hierarchy within the religious congregations themselves. Some orders worked with the wealthy while others worked predominantly with the poor. Although all provided much needed social services, the less wealthy indigenous orders were controlled by the bishops and therefore had less autonomy in their choice of apostolates than those controlled directly from Rome.

The early to mid-1900s was an era in Ireland when a stagnant society was presided over by a repressive and sexually obsessed Church from which the younger generation had to flee, a society where to be perceived as a good practicing Catholic brought social and economic advantage.[7] The woman's place was in the home, upholding the Catholic tradition. Career possibilities for single women were limited. In 1936, the then Minister for Industry and Commerce, Sean Lemass, prohibited the employment of women in industry. Large numbers of women emigrated rather than remain unemployed or dependent on relatives. Most of the Irish women emigrants were single and travelled alone. In 1960, more than half of the women who were aged 15 to 19 in 1942 were living outside Ireland.[8] There was, however, another alternative and that was to become a member of a religious congregation, which was a highly respectable calling but one that required a call from God to follow Him, commonly referred to as 'having a vocation'.

Until Vatican II the closed system that operated in convents saw women enter the convent and make an almost complete break with the world. The structures that held the system in stasis were set out in the rule and constitutions of the order, and included monastic enclosure, the three vows of poverty, chastity and obedience, and the acceptance of the almost godly status of the superior who 'knew' God's will.

In this period there was an interdependent relationship between the religious and the laity. The religious held and respected the spiritual values of the Church and carried out social services and education in return for a sufficient number of recruits to keep the institution operational. Religious saw themselves as being on a path to perfection and thereby superior to the laity on whose behalf they prayed and interceded with God, to ensure their salvation.[9] The laity needed the religious and they projected their goodness and holiness onto them. This left the religious in the invidious position of not being able to own their badness or humanity, in public at least. It was acted out unconsciously within the convent walls. The 'undesirables' in society, the Magdalens and the children in industrial schools, became likely receptacles for the bad projections of both the nuns and society. This added to their psychological burden and relieved the nuns and society of these feelings, but also deprived them of the chance of becoming whole, acknowledging the good and the bad.

The religious lost their special position of superiority following the universal call to holiness of Vatican II (*Lumen Gentium*). Since everyone was called to perfection leaving the convent was no longer seen as a failure and many left religious life.[10] Following the allegations of abuse, the perception of nuns changed from 'good and holy' to 'bad and abusive', and the State began to take control of social welfare institutions and education which has continued until the present.

This research sets out to explore religious life through the stories of the nuns, eight of whom spent up to thirty years of their lives living in the closed system that existed before the late 1960s and two who experienced the transition and the nuns' efforts at renewal and adaptation. The task, shared by the researcher in her empathic listening and understanding, is about constructing a story or narrative. It is the story of a self; a metaphorical telling of what once was fact. It is not a historical or factual account of events. Historical truth is impossible to access after the fact because it has been subjected to many interpretations and revisions.[11]

The underlying story of the hidden life of the convent is explored through the use of psychoanalytic concepts. It is a story that is present but not immediately represented other than in its effects.[12] Each nun's story begins with an introduction.

1

Teresa

'I never heard anyone complaining'

Introduction

At ninety-three years of age, Teresa, with her full faculties and a remarkable memory, represents an age group most of whom are no longer around. She entered the convent in 1930. She gives the impression that she sailed through life without having much input into the course of events, something that did not cause her any concern because it coincided with what she wanted. This rationalisation avoids the necessity for expressing any feelings.

She is very guarded in how she approaches her story. She is outspoken about her intention not to be negative. In her mind she has a script that can be followed and that will paint a good picture of the nuns, probably to vindicate their position and refute the 'very poor press' that they have been receiving. She is free to say whatever she wishes so she often makes a statement (the script) then contradicts it (the truth). Looking beneath the surface helps to decipher what she does not permit herself to say.

Her father, a farmer, built a two-storey slated house on the outskirts of a small country town around 1920, which suggests that they were a family of some means. Both her mother and father had cousins in religious life. Teresa's decision to enter the convent was based on chance, on synchronicity. Her mother's cousin who was a Mother General visited the school where Teresa was a pupil and somehow a bond was set up between them. She later learns that this woman is her cousin and interprets this woman's interest in her as a sign that she is destined for religious life. She laughs, enjoying the sense of mystery she creates, and she offers no further elaboration on this rather strange bond. It is somehow a bond of kinship, and Teresa follows her many relatives into religious life as if she were joining the family business. Her sibling followed her into the same order.

It was always the brightest who ended up in the convent. They were also enthusiastic and beautiful. Teresa aligns herself with this group. Their spiritual training in the novitiate consisted in reading Rodriquez, listening to lectures read by the Novice Mistress, and following the example of the older nuns. Rodriquez was a sixteenth century Spanish Jesuit who wrote The Practice of Christian and Religious Perfection. *He advocated blind obedience and has endured through the centuries for his admonition that nuns should plant cabbages upside down if told to do so by the superior. Teresa says at first that it was 'the daftest book', but then recants in favour of 'there were many good sentences in it'.*

Rodriquez advocated the obedience of St. Ignatius which was that of the professional soldier, who when his commanding officer gave a direction, obeyed without question, even to the death. The Jesuit was prepared even to disregard the evidence of his senses when the occasion required and his task was to save souls, in the service of the Church Militant. This interpretation of obedience was implemented in convents in a literal way. The young religious were being told to act in a certain way and not to reflect on this behaviour.

Initially, Teresa's life story has a military flavour. The headmistress in the convent secondary school was like a 'commander in chief'. The large group of novices walked in rows of three with the 'length of a stick' between them and then sat in the summer-house and darned their socks while they talked. Their holiday house had once been part of a British stronghold. On holidays the nuns were 'free and easy' with a lecture in the morning, recitation of the fifteen mysteries of the Rosary, going out in groups with packed lunches and returning at four o'clock for dinner! The 'cus-tom' was to be always engaged in something practical, polishing the brasses and the desks, and doing needlework at recreation. Idleness was not permitted. While other nuns speak of regimenta-tion, Teresa demonstrates it.

The nuns were highly respected by society. In the convent the young respected the old and the old were kind to the young. In her first assignment after her training Teresa tells how nice the nuns were to her, how they did their best to 'polish her off'. They wished to get rid of any of the dust that would have prevented her from being a 'good' nun. Did she actually find it quite difficult but cannot say it? Sometimes Teresa shows no feelings and other times she attributes feelings to others that might be her own. The only time she expresses a feeling is when she says she 'missed' her father. This was when he had died and she was transferred to her home town. It seems a bit harsh that the superiors waited until he died to send her back there. She says her mother was 'very happy' that they could now visit one another. Does this mean she was happy too but she cannot express it? She shows no anger at her parents for keeping her an extra year in primary school so that her teacher was enabled to get his diploma and 'she lost out' because she was too old to do what she wanted.

She says she was never lonely living with the two older women for eighteen years and that it passed 'quite pleasantly', before add-ing in the next breath that it was a 'difficult' and 'testing' time. Mother Aquinas, who was fond of her, permitted her to go to the library in the local post office and read any book she wished because she probably thought she was 'hemmed in'. She was also hemmed in by the habit the nuns were obliged to make (hem) and wear: 'it was a miracle a lot of people didn't die of heat' because of the weight of them. Maybe convent life was a bit suffocating for Teresa but she dare not give it voice. Although she says Aquinas was fond of her, she expresses no feeling for the old nun when she is transferred, against her wishes, after years of committing to one convent.

Teresa's mind was divided because she was overburdened trying to cope with the many demands on her time, but she does not complain to those in charge. Instead, she blames herself for not doing full justice to her teaching. She then consoles herself by claiming that the pupils did well enough but again modifies this by saying they would have done better if she had been better. The same thing happened in her present convent where she was bursar as well as teacher. She considers that to be unable to do 'two things' is her 'misfortune', and accuses herself of being 'scatterbrained'. She cannot be criticised for her self-recrimination but to lay the blame for overwork on the authorities might be dangerous.

She defends the order against the 'very poor press' they have received in recent years. There is conflict between what the 'orphans' are saying about not having been fed and what some sisters who taught them have told her. There was a one hundred and fifty acre farm attached to the convent and the children 'truly shared in the produce of that land'. She was not there and had no experience of the industrial school. This is a dilemma for her. Teresa is given to concrete thinking. What she observes is her gauge of truth. The nuns were women of 'highest ideals'; she never 'saw anything else'. They were all 'utterly content' as far as she 'could see'. The food was good because 'she never heard anyone com-

*plaining about it'. There was no one disgruntled or if there was
she didn't see it. She has now heard two conflicting stories and
she wasn't there to judge for herself. She is forced to come down
on one side and she chooses to defend those who for her are not
family 'but next door to it'.*

*Almost to compensate for defending something she is unsure
about she speaks of the one 'weakness' the nuns had, which was
that they paid more attention to their professional careers than
to their spiritual lives. In other words, the nuns got it wrong. They
failed in their primary purpose. Teresa conflates food and spirituality. Both are in short supply. The Church feast days are cel-
ebrated with lots of real food and the trifle is a work of art. The
expectation of spiritual sustenance is frustrated and supplanted
by food for the body just as the expectation of spirituality in the
convent is replaced by worldy pursuits, good in themselves but no
different to those pursued by people who have not taken vows to
follow Christ.*

*Having had the courage to make this astonishing criticism of
religious life she uses the views of others to make further criti-
cisms of pre-Vatican II life in the convent. Some say it was regimented, prevented personal growth and responsibility and that
there was probably a note of harshness. This is a covert criticism
of those in charge. She believes that people are only able to make
these comments in this age of enlightenment. Perhaps this fright-
ens her and she reverts to type and says that the nuns she dealt
with were 'decent spiritual women'.*

*She also reverts to her superior position by saying that she has
wider scope than her married sisters who are totally immersed
in and biased in favour of their own offspring. She takes a keen
interest in them and unlike her sisters she can 'take them all in'.
It was a common belief that nuns who were free from the worries
of marriage, parenthood and looking after material needs were*

able to be more inclusive and effective in their spiritual roles, and therefore superior to married people. She has no regrets.

Teresa is defended against presenting a true picture of her life, she is overtly supportive of the system in religious life, and her underlying story can be extrapolated by decoding what she says. She belongs to a generation that was part of an evolving Irish State, which was closely linked to an exponentially expanding Church, and she is willing to co-operate with both. She finds criticism of the nuns too much to bear.

Teresa's Story:

There were no awful complaints about school

Looking back it is true that I didn't make decisions about my life. I often think of it and if there was such a word as 'providence' (God's guidance) it entered my life anyway. What I wanted to do a lot of the time coincided with what was being done. A lot of people were very good friends, some of them extraordinary good friends.

I was born in 1912 and the school I attended was next door to my house. My father and mother had come into the parish. They had bought a place or my father had bought a place and had his house built. It was one of the first houses with slates and a second storey and the school being next door we went to it. The junior school was pleasant for us. It wasn't a very stressful education because the teachers changed quite frequently and learning came relatively easy to us. We didn't find it awful or there were no awful complaints about school. I should have left and gone to the convent but there was a young teacher there who was anxious to get his diploma and he was rather friendly with father and mother. I suppose he was anxious to have somebody to keep the flag flying so I stayed there. Then I went off to the convent and the reason I went there was because my mother had a first cousin there. She used to call her Birdie and I didn't know she was a nun at all.

The headmistress was more like a commander in chief

Everyone was most respectful of the nuns, at that time, and indeed they deserved it. The superior in her great enthusiasm for education had the spelling book. Now you never heard of the spelling book but it had Latin and Greek roots and spelling. She insisted, much to the principal's annoyance, that the spelling book should be done every day. So we had Latin and Greek roots and all that. There was a young nun doing her starting examination. The inspector came and it was a fair day. There was no school on a fair day, except the girls for examination. It was too dangerous to be passing through cattle and horses. So there was a class of us girls in the school and the nun for her examination was downstairs polishing her brasses and polishing the desks as was the custom. A gentleman came in and said he was looking for 'an Siuir Carmel' (Sister Carmel).

'Well that's me.'

'I'm coming to examine your work.'

'Well, there's no class.'

But the headmistress went downstairs and she manufactured a class out of all of us and we did the *Flight of the Earls* and it was marvellous. Carmel didn't have much to do and he thought she was great.

I had a very happy time at school there. At that time preparatory college had come into being. Maybe I should tell you the way the principal worked. Well, she had about seventy girls in her class and she had them in sections: county scholarship, preparatory college, post office, and clerical officers, and at that time there was Easter scholarship for girls who went to training. So she started in the morning with the county scholarships and they went through their paces and she took out the years' papers before that and set them down to work. She went on with the next and the next and the next, she was more like a commander in chief. They were all going places. Because I stayed back in primary school I was too old for the county scholarship so the only thing left for me was to do the Easter scholarship and go to training from that. It used to be called the 'King's scholarship', but after the Easter Rising it was called the Easter scholarship. I set my sights on that. And lo and behold, the Department of Education, in their wisdom, said they wouldn't call anyone to training outside the preparatory colleges, so I lost out at both ends.

After some time I heard of a rural domestic science school and I thought that was my delight because I was from the country and it was lovely. Then I would go to the Munster Institute but the principal said, 'You cannot go to the Munster Institute without matriculation because you'd be going on to the university, if you so wished.'

'But I don't think we could do matriculation here, that we'd be allowed.' We were allowed and I did matriculation and got it.

Destined for religious life

I didn't know at the time that my mother's first cousin was the Mother General of all the convents. She came to visit our school and she didn't know me or I didn't know her but somehow a bond was struck between us. She asked the headmistress who I was, and she told her who I was but she didn't know there was any relationship. But another cousin came in that evening to see the Mother General and she told her of this child she saw today and she said, 'Do you know who that is? That's Kate O'Connor's daughter.' She was my mother and she was a first cousin of the Mother General so from that day out, it seemed that I was destined for the religious life instead of the agricultural life. So that's how I landed in in the convent.

At the time there were about forty in the noviceship. They were all young, enthusiastic, intelligent and beautiful and we had a most happy time. The order had two schools at that time. They got the brains of the country and strange to say the firsters (the brightest) always ended up in the noviceship. That seemed to be an unwritten tradition and it went on for a number of years. So the noviceship was a very lively place and a very intellectual place, with very bright people. Well our Novice Mistress had a middle class education and she was an intelligent woman. Her talks were quite up to date. She was a very decent woman and very spiritual woman. She certainly did her best to form us in the formation of the day.

I never heard anyone complaining

The noviceship was a building apart and recreation was separate but we had our meals together with the other nuns and the food was good. I never heard anyone complaining about it. And we had great reverence for the people older than us and they were kind to us and good to us. Then we went to school, just to observe teaching, and we might get jotters to correct sums for first class, second class and on upwards. On a Saturday one of the teachers brought in her class and all who were going for teaching went down and she gave a lesson and we commented. Sometimes someone might be called out to finish the lesson so it wasn't right to say we got no training in teaching. We did. Before we went to training proper, we were not in school 'red raw', as you'd say. We did have training and very good training because the schools had a very high standard. We corrected jotters and the nuns encouraged us and were lovely to us and so were the teachers so I haven't anything horrific to say about religious life. They were all decent, well-motivated women. And had the highest ideals and I never saw anything else.

Everyone I knew in the noviceship was content. And they were great and they were very brilliant and they were great fun and they were utterly content as far as I could see. And you could laugh; I mean nobody prevented you from laughing. If you had two good-humoured people one each side of you, you would laugh at something. People were very witty and you can't bury that; it would come to the surface and you'd have to laugh at the most extraordinary times. Vatican II hadn't happened when I was in the novitiate or for years after and it was unheard of to hear of anybody leaving the convent. A nun left because she was ill or for some reason like that but she never left to liberate herself because she didn't want to. She felt that hers was the better part. Some people, of course, would be quite negative and you'd really want to get both sides of the story.

We did spiritual reading after school. I suppose it was meditation or contemplation or whatever, in the right sense of the word. But the books were very old fashioned, Rodriquez if you ever heard of him. It was a very old fashioned book. The virtues of poverty chastity and obedience were pointed out and discussed in a very old fashioned manner. It was the daftest book you could imagine. He wanted people to plant cabbages upside down, if the superior told them to, blind obedience it was called. As a farmer's daughter's I didn't take him seriously. Well, maybe all of it wasn't daft; there were many good sentences in it. In my three years of noviceship there weren't any what you would call up to date spiritual books. And at any rate we weren't encouraged to read them. I got a present of one. Unfortunately, I cannot recall the name of it now but it was quite nice, quite spiritual and I was permitted to use it.

We had two lectures in the day, or what were called lectures. The Novice Mistress read from what would be a more modern book. She read it and she questioned us on it. There would be morning and evening instructions, and when the superior came she questioned us on the Catechism of the vows and the holy rule, the rulebook. And that would be our spiritual training and the example of each other and the example of the community of which we were a part.

We walked around the grounds in groups of three

Lunch was very light, a cup of tea, bread and butter and eggs, and after that we went in threes to say the rosary. We said the fifteen mysteries of the Rosary walking around the walks and then we came back to the noviceship and sat around and did some needlework. Chiefly we made the coif and guimp (headdress), which were handmade. We were all around a big table and we showed mother what we were doing; sure we all knew how to rip anyway! We got on nicely and it was pleasant enough, there wasn't much giddy talk or anything like that. You know, it was serious. Then recreation was after dinner. We walked around the grounds in groups of three. There was a large group; the first three would only be the length of a stick away then the next three and the next three. Sometimes we sat in the summerhouse and if we had stockings to darn we took them out of our big sleeves and darned away while the conversation was on. We weren't meant to be idling.

The habits were made apart. There was a workroom and a staff there of three or four and one old nun. They were trained in sewing and your whole outfit was ready for your reception or your profession. You got your white veil at reception and at first profession you were given a black veil. The clothing of the day was extremely heavy. It was wool serge and you had the pleated habit and under it was an underskirt of the same material. And you had a very heavy undergarment I suppose what the French called the chemise and a bodice and a foundation garment and the stockings, nylons hadn't come in yet, were wool or cotton. It was a miracle a lot of people didn't die of heat, especially in summer. The clothes were no lighter in summer than they were in winter. So that was that.

We had, as I mentioned, a very intellectual company so there was plenty of wisdom, humour and all that talent. Some would be practicing their music for music exams doing classical pieces and others would be practicing speech and drama or some other thing. And then others would be preparing for examinations that would occur. You had to get your *Teastas* (certificate) to teach Irish and your 'bi-lingual' before you went to training.

We had rising at five-thirty, Morning Prayer and then Mass. We were, as I told you, well catered for. Everybody had an egg for breakfast. I never see anybody eating an egg now. On our own feast day, that is the feast of our patron, we got pancakes for lunch. The feasts of the Church were kept well. We had the usual breakfast and then dinner and a very nice trifle. They used to make a very good trifle. It was a work of art. You had that on that day.

The sisters should have a holiday house

I was in the noviceship for three years and then I went to a branch house after my first profession. And from 1937 to 1939 I was in training and then I spent a year after training in that branch house. I taught fifth class. I was in the same room as the headmistress. It was quite a big room and she had her class at one end and I had a class at the other. She had the senior classes, sixth, seventh and eighth. The eighth were preparing for examinations. Some were preparing for the county scholarship, preparatory college or the post office and then there was the rank and file of the class. The headmistress was a very conscientious teacher and she would spend a lot of her time with the non-examination, the non-intellectual, pupils. It was a wonderful experience to teach in the same room as her. I was there so she could keep an eye on me. I got on fairly well with fifth class. I was happy and they were happy.

I was a member of the community then. The headmistress and I went on a long walk on Sundays. At recreation we listened to gramophone records. It was chiefly classical music, the Irish music hadn't come into its own at that time. There would be some songs, chiefly John McCormack's, and that's it really. There were about ten nuns and they were all very good to me and kind and did their best to polish me off.

The bishop, at the time, thought the sisters should have a holiday house. There was an old British stronghold by the sea with two coastguard residences. They were in a ruinous state for some years. He came to the superior and told her to buy these two and have them restored as a seaside holiday house. That was done. There was a small school at the back of the house and the principal teacher was retiring. She was a Miss Murphy and the bishop suggested that a sister should be offered to the school so that there would be some little bit of money coming in the whole year, other than what would come in during the holiday season. A sister was appointed. She was Sister Patrick from Dublin. She had been trained before she entered and she took over the school. There were between fifty and sixty children in it and there was an assistant teacher and herself. It was like all rural schools, quite primitive and she had it painted. It was all one room when she arrived and she put up a wooden partition so the second teacher had a room of her own. She was there for from 1929 until 1940 and she was of retiring age in 1940. She was an independent woman and she told the superior that she had reached retiring age and there was no one in the convent except Mother Aquinas and Sister Peter and domestic staff, a couple of girls. So there was much searching around and it was thought that I'd be acceptable because my cousin, the previous superior, was a great friend of Mother Aquinas. I don't know what kind of divine inspiration that was but it seemed that Mother Aquinas had some kind of a *grá* (fondness) for me. Down I went at twenty-five and I was eighteen years there.

I lived with Mother Aquinas, who was eighty, and Sister Patrick, who was reaching seventy, and that was the community. And I lived through that quite pleasantly. I didn't have any friends there outside the convent. My confessor asked me about that one time. My interest was in the children. I didn't feel the need of friendship. I was on my own, more or less, but I was never lonely. I suppose separation is an attitude of mind really. I think that you can be quite close to people and be a distance away from them. I mean in your thoughts and affections and even their influence on you can be from a distance. It was a difficult time, a testing time, to be on your own but there was a branch of the county library in the small rural post office and Mother Aquinas told me I could go up and choose my books. She never said, 'What did you get or what did you not get', and I read every book in the house. I was young and I suppose she thought I was hemmed in. Then the holiday time came around, the gang appeared again and I had lots of company. And for my own holiday I went to a small convent because my sister was there.

I didn't give my full attention to school

In the school I had the boys and girls and Sister Patrick didn't. She belonged to the era where she had sufficient Irish to satisfy the Department of Education but the children became quite good at Irish after my arrival. Then the time came for Mother Aquinas and Sister Patrick to be transferred. Mother Aquinas had the idea that as a founder member she wouldn't be changed but she was. They were very good administrators. Sure they were, it was very orderly. Other nuns came and they had no experience of taking in people for holidays making lists and all that. I would be called on to assist at that too so I have to confess that I didn't give my full attention to school. I'm sure it suffered a bit anyway. Our superior hadn't good health and then the neighbours would be coming in to borrow a barrow or a shovel or something else. They'd come up to the school to me so my mind was there and I feel that I should have been more sensible and told the governing body at the time that no one can do two things or more at one time. That was my fault. I didn't do the pupils full justice but they got on well and they did well in life. But, of course, they would have done better if I had done better.

Everyone got a fortnight's holiday there during the summer and that was a free and easy time. Well you had a lecture in the morning; we said the Rosary, the fifteen mysteries, probably. Other than that you walked out in groups and no one told you what time to be in. You set off on your own, the packed lunches were simple, bread and jam, and you came back to dinner at four o'clock. So that was my experience all through.

It was time to give me a change

So I was there from 1940 until 1958. My father had died in February 1958. The superior thought it was time to give me a change and she did. I was sent to my home town and I was mistress of schools there. It was always a lovely town to teach in and although they say that no prophet is accepted in his own country the people accepted me. My father wasn't there and I missed him because I was very close to him. It was a great consolation to my mother and to the rest of the family that I was near them. I could see my mother any time I liked. She could come to me or I could go over to her. It was just three miles away. I suppose she was very happy and had a certain amount of pride, in that I was principal of the school at that time. At that time there was that respect for the religious.

It wasn't a good time economically for the country. Nuns used to come around from different places fostering vocations. In the school the folding doors would be opened and the senior classes would gather. The nuns would tell them about their congregations. We jokingly said we should send out for the young farmers and let them up on the platform and let the classes in because no young men were getting married at that time. There might be a year when there was no marriage in the parish. It's different now, they don't bother getting married, but these men didn't take that road, they stayed single. The country was suffering so we were going to give a platform to the men but that never happened. I was in this convent for six years and then I was moved again.

The orphanage had just closed

I came here and I'm forty years here. This house and land were donated to the bishop. He asked the sisters to take over and have the Industrial School here. They came and the nun who came was Mother Alphonsus and she was an aristocrat from Castlemanor. She had two brothers who were priests and a sister a nun. The family came to the agreement that their home, which was quite a large estate, was to be sold and each of the four get their share of the inheritance. With her share Mother Alphonsus bought one hundred and fifty acres of land to feed the orphans who now say they weren't fed at all. She had seven men sow oats, wheat, barley and vegetables. She had sheep, cattle and cows. There was a dairy here also and a bakery and the children truly shared in the produce of that land. The stories now in circulation are quite different but these are the facts. From what I hear Mother Alphonsus was confined to a wheelchair at the end of her days, but she was wheeled down to the school and to the farmyard every day to see how things were going. She had nothing on her mind as important as the feeding of these children. When I came here the orphanage had just closed so I had no experience of it, but I know some sisters who taught in it and they say that the superiors who had to do with the children were very dedicated. They had schoolbags for them, they had their books and their names on them and they got expert teaching in class. In these days they were at school with the local children. Now where do we go from here?

Some say the system had been regimented

I was bursar here and you know no one can be doing two things so that's my great misfortune. I was a little bit scatterbrained but again any community I lived in was grand. There was no one disgruntled or if there was I didn't see it. They were not supposed to be family but they were next door to it. I would say the one weakness we had was that we were probably more oriented to the professional side of our lives than to the spiritual side. While we did say our prayers and all the rest of it, again I'm only speaking for myself. It didn't occur to us that our first priority was the spiritual. Once you knew how you were to spend your life, what your profession was to be, either nursing or teaching, you gave a lot of your thought to that. Would you be a success in the classroom? A lot of your energy went into that. You had exams to do. If you went to training, you hoped you'd do well, and probably there were times when that aspect outweighed the spiritual side. So I suppose that's the reason why we're told that the contemplatives get vocations now because career prospects won't enter into it.

After Vatican II people would say that the system had been regimented and that it had prevented growth, personal growth, personal responsibility, and they would possibly say there had been a note of harshness. This would not occur in the early years. It would occur in the years of enlightenment. I feel genuinely that I was dealing with very decent, spiritual women. Within the last twenty years or somewhat less we got a very poor press. Well to me it always felt that a lot of it was totally undeserved. No nun that I ever knew would conform to what I read of in the press.

I have no regrets

Nuns and convent were good for people at the time. And they were right for our young country and our young country owes them an awful lot. Nuns were well thought of. It felt good to be a nun and for the family to have a nun. I know my sisters who have grandchildren are totally immersed in them. They think that there are no children like their children, but I can take a very keen interest in them all. I say I have a wider scope than the grandmothers because I can take them all in.

The day of large communities is over and what must happen now is that the few people who are left will have to say to the lay people, 'Well we're handing it over to you'. I think that's an evolution and I have no regrets.

2

Nora

'Never do that to anybody again'

Introduction

Telling her life story is a voyage of discovery for Nora who is eighty-six years of age. By allowing herself to speak freely she discovers things she didn't know she knew. She calls her defences her 'sins of omission'. She had insight but felt powerless and turned a blind eye. Turning a blind eye is one of the ways in which contradictory versions of reality are able to coexist. It is a means of knowingly deciding not to know.[13] It will keep facts conveniently out of sight and will allow the individual to know and not to know simultaneously, which can lead to distortions and misrepresentations of the truth.[14] The reason for turning a blind eye is the fear of the truth and a reality that cannot be faced.[15] Nora has now let her knowledge into her conscious mind and has to deal with her regret.

She grew up in the Gaeltacht where her family, like those around her, struggled with life but never went hungry. She saw education rather than emigration as a way forward. She attended a local convent primary school and was awarded a scholarship to boarding school. She was later awarded a university scholarship.

Nora's sister became a nun in England but before she entered she spent ten years working to pay for her brother's education and to help the family. Nora also helped the family but in a different way. She made a covenant with God that He would bless her family if she became a nun. For this sacrifice the Gospel promises a hundredfold reward in this world, and salvation in the next. The Church promised that it was not only oneself that was saved, but also everyone for whom one prayed and there was also the real possibility of becoming a saint. There were also more mundane aspects to her decision. Her friend invited her to come with her and Nora set up a lottery to decide. She made a Mass novena. Implicit in this superstitious act was the belief that if the priest failed to turn up on at least one of the nine days, she did not have a vocation. She projected the responsibility for her decision on to the priest who, of course, was unaware of the part he played.

When she was ten or eleven years old, in play with her sister, Nora decided she would give up her babies to become a nun. She had somehow taken in that not having babies was a good idea, and this is not surprising when one considers the hardships suffered by many women in Ireland at the time. They reared large families with less than adequate resources. There may, also, have been an unconscious component to her decision. The nuns offered advancement and opportunity to the less privileged, and one wonders if girls who benefitted from free education felt that they were obliged to repay the debt by sacrificing their lives for others and joining the nuns in their work.

Nora recalls some of the injustices of the convent: the social class system, the prohibition on visiting a mother with a baby and the excessive work regime. She never refused to do what she was told. Constant busyness left little time for reflection and deprived the sisters of a critical function necessary for maturation. She did not speak about these things, which she now sees as her 'sins of omission'. Instead she somatised her feelings and suffered many illnesses. Nora had insight, but of necessity turned a blind eye and became blind. She could not allow her knowledge into her conscious mind. To know might have demanded action, maybe even leaving the convent, and she acknowledges she could never have brought herself to this point, although she thought about it many times. She felt she had nowhere to go and no one to go to. She was far from home in a strange place. Living in the convent meant coming to terms with the established and the unquestioned, and accepting the established without question. In order to survive, one had to turn a blind eye to what was unacceptable.

The discrimination against the lay sisters made her angry because they reminded her of her family. Originally, lay sisters came into convents as servants of the choir/community sisters. They were usually from poor backgrounds and were unable to pay a dowry. Nora was told that they were not educated and there was no mention of the dowry. The rule demanded that all should have compassion and love for the poor, so how could the convent, then, treat the poor nuns as domestic slaves? It would seem as if poverty as a reason for their plight had to be denied and be replaced by a lack of education. Bright girls like Nora who could not afford education received it free from the nuns so the implication may be that these lays sisters were incapable of being educated. Perhaps because they were not so bright they would not question their position in upholding the social class system.

Nora feels ashamed of some of the practices, especially the confession of faults and the importance attached to the breaking of an egg-cup; the breaking of the great silence to speak with a friend who was being sent home because Nora was deemed to be too friendly with her and the constant vigilance to ensure there was no sexual contact or even friendship between the nuns. To defend against the pain they made fun of things and used coded language to communicate things like the superior's mood on the day. This begs the question of Nora's coded language. What cannot be said?

The story of the mother and her new baby is so distressing that self-censorship kicks in. Nora is shocked by her unconscious. The fear of speaking, without censorship, is so strong that she wants to withdraw what she has said. She thinks of her home, of her mother who delivered babies. Previously she had to deal with her identification with the lay sisters and now she identifies with her mother. She has renounced motherhood and a mother's life in favour of the religious life. The rules of this new life are in conflict with mother's life and the family's interest in newborn babies. These thoughts are painful, but she does not condemn the nun who refused to visit the mother but blames the system, the rule. When she returns to the convent she does not speak to anyone about the incident, and it is only now that she speculates on the reason for this prohibition. She thinks that this rule related to the vow of chastity but she is unsure.

Contact with newborn babies brings one in contact with one's maternal instinct and with thoughts of sex. There is a possibility of becoming 'broody' and desiring a baby of one's own, and in the convent such a temptation had to be guarded against. Until 1936, Sisters were not allowed to study medicine or midwifery.[16] At the time, mothers who had given birth could not return to the Church until they had received a special blessing. They had to be 'churched' so, in the mind of the Church, birth was unclean. The Church's view may have infected this convent with a fear of motherhood.

Nora is experiencing an emotional release in freely expressing what comes to her mind, and she has some regrets about holding on to things in the past, of allowing her rebellion to be 'inside'. She speaks of nuns 'slapping' children in the industrial school and at-

tributes it to the 'very holy silence' that was anything but holy. Feelings and emotions influence thinking, which in turn influence behaviour. Speaking, 'letting it out', helps to clarify thinking, although feelings have a far bigger impact on behaviour than thinking does.[17] *The nuns working in the industrial schools were untrained, discriminated against and at the bottom of the social ladder in the convent. They were likely to have had doubts about their own value, and taken in feelings of worthlessness projected by the children. If they felt under attack or disrespected by these children they were likely to have responded with a rage that was out of proportion, and beaten the children without thinking and perhaps regretted it later. To talk about it would have made them vulnerable, and in a system where everyone was striving for perfection this would have been unthinkable, so the cycle continued.*

Nora has learned from her experience in the convent. She recently re-experiences the alienation of 1934 when she is uprooted from her home and friends and moved to a convent forty miles away but this time there is a different outcome. She is able to make her feelings known to the authorities; her rebellion is no longer inside.

Nora's Story:

We were struggling with life

I came from the Gaeltacht. Yes, and I knew a lot about the bog and the sea and the mountains and lakes and hills and I knew little about nuns or about life abroad.

I'm one of six children. Now all are dead except one, a sister called Molly who is married and has nine children and great-grandchildren.

In retrospect, our family was struggling with life. You wouldn't call us poor, we were never hungry or that. At the time we were like all the others round about us. We were just day-to-day living really and we had no high notions of going to school unless we happened to get a scholarship. The nuns in the primary school were instrumental in helping others like me leave the place we were in. Education now was the way to get on in life, not so much emigration as working the head and getting a scholarship.

Back in 1934 I got a scholarship and I was guided by one of the nuns to go to an English-speaking boarding school about fifty miles from home. There I spent five years with its ups and downs. I loved school, but I was really lost as a boarder. We spoke Irish at home. My English was not good. We had to pick up a few words of English. Naturally, I could understand quite a bit of it but the talking of it and the speaking of it, the accent, would not be up to the standard of my co-students. I suffered a bit that way. I had good Irish and somehow I never lost the love of it or the respect for it. So off I went to boarding school, very raw, and I spent five years there.

I felt they were taking advantage of me

It was a huge break for a Gaeltacht girl to go to boarding school. While the nun was teaching History and Geography, I used to think, wouldn't I be just as well off in South Africa. That was loneliness you know, loneliness. Lessons were not an awful lot of trouble to me. I liked school. But these thoughts would come across my mind when I wasn't expecting them. As I've said, my English wasn't up to the standard of the girls around me and at that particular time in the 1930s there were girls there who were a bit snobbish. They loved to hear me talking. We used to read at meals and they got me up in the first term to read in English. I remember a small stool and I standing on it, shaking. I felt they were taking advantage of me. The nun in charge wouldn't have been the best for that kind of thing. You know, she was all right, but if the girls asked to hear me reading English, as a bit of a joke, she would do nothing. My entire first year I felt it in here, in my heart. The nun wouldn't understand at all. She wouldn't. I never cared for her, the poor creature, but she wouldn't have that understanding. The girls wanted this. It was cruel for me. I should have refused but I wouldn't dream of it. There wasn't anybody there to say, 'you shouldn't ask her, she's only a month here and it's English. Why didn't you ask her to read a bit of Irish.' There wasn't one. But I felt it. It was unfair. It was making a laugh, giving a chance to others to hear my accent and to laugh. School now, school would be different, quite different, the sisters in school were not like that. But this sister now, I don't want to give her name. There was a bit of pride in me. Oh, I felt that intensely and it has remained with me and I talk about it with the same bit of feeling that I had then.

It's the alienation

My father and mother, the creatures, I used to go home to them, but I do think, as I said about South Africa, it was a mistake that I had to go so far away. And to have English spoken all round me was hard. It was hard. It was. It was the big break. It was too much of a break to have gone away, at that particular time. As I say, the house was small when I came back. I had friends though. I had other girls, great friends altogether, you know. I would say it's alienation. That now was a huge break.

Our letters used to be read. Didn't I write a sly letter to my mother to ask for something, to be as good as the other girls. I forget now what it was. She wrote back to me, 'if you write another sly letter to me I'll bring you home'. She didn't like a sly letter. She didn't, well she wouldn't have known that my letters were read. There was this distance between the life I was leading and the life I was brought up to at home. I told her in the letter what I had done. I needn't have told her. She wouldn't like her daughter to do sly things. Now, the poor woman never went to a secondary school, she had a national school education. She had a *seanfhocal* (old saying) for every instance, to teach us a lesson. The nurses now and the teachers and all that came to the area, maybe Irish wouldn't be so fluent with them. They made their way to my mother because she was so social, the creature. The door was open for everyone. And she had time to talk, poor thing.

I gave my babies away

When, in 1939, I did the Leaving Certificate the war had broken out on the first of September. It came in on our radio. In my Leaving Certificate year I was sitting at the back of the class with Bríd, who is now also an old nun like myself, and she told me she was entering the convent and she said, 'I think you should go too'. What did I do? I made a novena, nine days, a Mass novena, and during the novena I was hoping that the priest wouldn't come one of the days so that I would break it, but mind you, he came every day. I decided to enter. There was more than that. At the back of my head I was worried about the family. How would they struggle with life? I felt that perhaps if I did something, a sacrifice, get nearer to Christ, He would bless them. Nobody in the house knew, I'm just saying it now but just before I go ahead, a little story about when we were younger.

Molly and myself were making dolls, rag dolls, and we had up to a dozen, I think, and we were hugging them and all the rest of it. I was ten or eleven. And I don't know why, I didn't know anything about nuns, but I said to her,

'Molly, you can have my dolls.'

'Why?'

'I'm going to be a nun.'

'Well, I'd like to be a nun too but I'd like to have a baby first.'

33

She said this as she took one of the dolls. I'm telling you that vocation is something that's mysterious in a way. It's a call, without a doubt, for me and I say for those who lived at my time it was a call. I'd related the story to Molly and she had forgotten it but I keep it. I hold it and I tell it now as something that explains that a vocation goes back long before you give it thought. And she said, 'I'd like to be a nun too but I'd like to have a baby first'. I gave my babies away.

You'll never get out again

I entered in early September 1939, a most beautiful day, and the evening before I went out alone and looked at the sun setting. This is perfectly true. I looked at the sun setting, could almost see it now. I looked at it and looked at it and the tears came down because I thought I'd never see a sunset again. Absolutely so, and I can still see that sunset now.

Jimmy came with us, he was the driver, my mother, Lord have mercy on her, and my first cousin and myself. That's all that came. My older sister, Máirín, was in the Civil Service. She wasn't with us. She was working. She told me later on in life, when she became a nun herself, that she went to Knock, praying for me and for the family. On the way Jimmy said, 'Oh this is a lovely place, there's the lake there and the mountains and we'll take a snap'. Imagine, we took a snap and I never saw it. They thought they could never send it to me.

We arrived at the convent about five o'clock in the evening and everything was taken out of the car. I forgot an umbrella that I bought in Brown Thomas and Jimmy went back for it. 'Take this,' said he, 'because you'll never get out again.' We went in. There were four others in before me. We got tea and the whole regimentation, I wasn't used to it but we behaved rightly. So Jimmy, my first cousin and my mother left.

That sunset, the pond, and the wild lilies we plucked beside the lake – we went across the mountain to get them – they're the things I was lonely for and the *céihlí* (visiting) of course, and my friends, Máire, Áine, Tilly, and the rest of them. It was an absolute surrender, a word I didn't even know nor did it occur to me, but it was real, absolute. Surrender to all things that my heart craved so much. I carried them in my heart. I had to face this new life, big house, and people with their eyes cast down, people looking at you sideways, sizing you up. You know the way my heart was so much in between. Well anyhow, it would take a whole book to describe that.

It was the first time I was touching grandeur

So six of us entered. I was the fifth on that day, and a fortnight after Tess entered. She was a bit older than us. She had spent seven years teaching. She had gone on a holiday to France. She was tall, thin, you would look up to her, not because of her height only, but there was a great polish about her. She came in late September. Now one of the other postulants came down to us and said, 'Oh, there's a new postulant and she has a gorgeous hat from France. It will be lovely for the concert after Christmas.' We each had brought a case with our things and some of the cases were nicer than others. We were putting marks on them when Tess came with a big case, everything somewhat grander than we had. And I was feeling an inferiority complex, not saying anything, walking away, laughing when I should, doing everything, but inside me I was feeling inferior, not that I should, because Tess was lovely. We were great friends until she died. But you see, it was the first time really I was touching grandeur because she had very grand things.

I was thinking how humble my things were. My blankets, we got them from the sheep ourselves. We got them, whatever you call this, turned them into thread, in our own place, and we made blankets of them. Therefore they weren't like the posh blankets that Tess had. Now I was passing no remarks, some were saying that they were lovely. But inside of me, I wasn't jealous now, more this inferiority. There was no need for me to feel it. Tess was lovely but I was very new. It was a new life, another look at life out of that trunk and I remember it so distinctly. Just look what I'm talking about, sunsets, snaps, going into the convent, my mother leaving. She was probably proud of me. Then our noviceship began and Tess and I became the best of friends. I was with her at the end of everything and I have more letters from her than I have from anybody else, short ones, but letters.

They told me they were lay sisters

I was there, very raw if you like in many ways. But I saw women round about me, with little white aprons on them and they'd take that apron off and put on a check one. I asked, 'Why are these nuns wearing an apron?' They told me they were lay sisters. I had to get to know what a lay sister meant. And they told me they possibly hadn't the chance we had and therefore they were looked upon as lay sisters. I felt in my heart for them, and for a few days I thought, I'll become a lay sister to fight my way. It's true. I didn't. That's the way I was feeling then, touching wealth, grandeur, but at the same time I came down to my roots. And when I saw these nuns beautiful, all so lovely to me, with the little apron, not going to office with us, not having Mary in their name, not being with us, this is the way I felt, not talking so much but thinking that I'd ask to become a lay sister. I didn't do it. It's one of the many things I didn't do. It's a point I'm going to bring out, these sins of omission, call them whatever, but I did feel it and inside of me, would you call it anger? I don't know. That's the way I felt. They're just like the people I left behind me. I didn't do it but I had it here in my heart. Well, to bring that point out really, there was a difference between what they called a community sister and a lay sister and the ordinary person from my background feeling this goodness all about me, this was a blot on the loving picture that I had before me.

The Novice Mistress, too, was a bit of a grandee, but lovely. I loved her. She had to teach us custody of the eyes, how to sit up straight in the chair, how to speak properly, and our manners and prayer. She was a woman of prayer, lovely watching her at the Stations of the Cross. Now even though she was a bit grand and all that, I felt she was holy. She was somebody you'd like to be like, even though she might be a bit grand.

They'd be telling it in the pub

On our first day we were sitting down in our chairs and the novice mistress was up at the top and there was a row of us postulants and a nun, who was only two years ahead of us, went out to the middle of the room and kissed the floor, and said, 'I'm very sorry for breaking an eggcup yesterday'. An eggcup! Well I went back again in my mind to my place at home. What if they heard this! They'd be telling it in the pub. I'm talking about something now that shows that we were in need of a change. Isn't that really what I'm at? With the wisdom of old age it's coming to me now talking to you.

Particular friendship

You weren't supposed to go in at night to talk to anyone or anything like that. But now, I remember Sister Carmel who was my companion and I thought they were going to send her home. My heart was broken and I said, 'Tell them I'll go home instead of you'. That's the way we could feel for one another and you'd break the rule to do that. To us it wasn't breaking anything. There were rules but they were silly, really. Some of them were really silly. I was going to go home over this. I had a relationship, a particular friendship and the Novice Mistress said, 'Oh you could get too fond of one another,' and I said, 'What's in that?' and I was hor-rified. But then I went with it. There was no explanation. When I thought of it, later on in life, I knew it was wrong because friendship is a wonderful thing. But we were thrown together as a crowd of women. We had given up so much, you know, and they were watching. Well, not watching, these were part of the rules to help you, to protect you, to keep you from getting too near anyone. I wonder was there a need? Oh yes, the Novice Mistress told me, the creature, that I was too fond of Carmel and when I told Carmel she said, 'We'll begin now.' It was a cod (fun). It was fun. I didn't see it then but that's the way, we made fun of it. You see humour is a marvellous thing. It was humour helped us. Because when we'd come together, we'd laugh at it. Humour is gone today. Maybe it's not as necessary today. Humour was wonderful, wonderful. And very often we might only have one word and that was enough. Everyone knew. We'd say, 'How is her dimity today?'

'Oh it went that way.'

'Oh here?'

'Yes, that's it.'

Talk about the Da Vinci code! We had a code, which was wonderful.

Maybe I shouldn't be saying this

We had a nun and she used to do visitation and then we postu-lants were sent out with her to our life of meeting the poor. She was lovely now and good to the people. A wee little girl ran across to her, passing me by, and said, 'Mammy wants you'.

And she said, 'What does Mammy want me for?'

And the child said, 'She has a baby,' and I'm back now in the 1940s, and she said, 'We don't go to the house on those occasions'.

Well, I nearly turned back and went home. But this was a beautiful nun, loved the poor, whatever money she got she gave to them. This was the rule. Maybe I shouldn't be saying this. You can cancel it. The things that are coming back to me! That's what she said. She said it nicely. I was almost going to turn back. I nearly did it. I didn't.

I almost did on that occasion because my mother was a handy-woman. She'd be called out at any time to bring little babies into the world. And we'd stay up at night to ask her, 'Is it a boy or a girl?' That sister was kind. People gave so much money that the nuns had plenty of it for the poor but this was a rule that we nuns didn't go to a mother who had a baby. Maybe the baby was born there. I got the idea about the baby being small, maybe newly born. Well, why am I talking about them? Erase it. This is coming from somewhere. It isn't the sister but that she couldn't do it. It's about the rules, isn't it? I share this and it's against myself. I'm trying to get to know myself now in my old age. I didn't go back and start telling the sisters I left behind me, or my own sisters. I had it in here in my heart. You see, that's important. I see now. I didn't see it at that time, this not opening out. My rebellion was inside. I don't remember making any comment. Possibly I went into the chapel and did the little things we were supposed to do. But anyhow, I'm doing the same thing again now. I hope I finish with it.

You'll love the rebel in me

I remember the common life that wasn't always common. During Advent we didn't get parcels or letters, they were kept until Christmas day. On Christmas day the novices, the young ones, distributed them. Some people would get the height of parcels and letters and some would get very few or none at all. So much so that one sister wrote to herself. Look at the things I remember. You know, you'll love the rebel in me.

In 1942, it was wartime, I had the three years done 1939 to 1942. I had the black veil and the vows taken, the first vows. I had a scholarship now to go to the university so they sent me to another convent. I don't even remember the bus I came on but I remember coming in to the convent. All the nuns so nice, coming up to welcome me and to make me feel at home but I heard one of them say, 'She has soft hands, she won't be staying'. Look what I'm thinking of. I did see the welcome. I was lost in the welcome, but the little whisper that I shouldn't have heard, I remember it.

When time came for the university oh, lovely story. I went on the train. As I got into the carriage there were two men there from the boat who must have been working in England and they were coming home and they had their pipes, very respectable, very respectable. 'This is a nun,' one of them said to the other, 'so we can't even smoke now.'

Then, after a while I said, 'You have permission to smoke,' and they pulled in their legs and said, 'You have Irish, God bless you,' and we were just three in one. We had a great old chat in Irish.

There were the little eyes looking up at me

I had four happy years at university, no worries whatsoever. Helping everyone, you know, anything to pass the time and I never missed anything, did all the reading and everything. Got through. And the minute I began to teach, from the first day, I was a totally different woman. I went totally serious. This was life really. I had to be responsible now. I was supposed to teach them. I honestly changed overnight from being a happy-go-lucky person to a very serious-minded, conscientious one, wanting to help those who needed my help. And every day of my teaching life I loved. We had ups and downs. We had misunderstandings. We had all that but I loved the children and my teaching life, every day of it. If I had the energy or if I could live life over again I would do it again. Now I won't tell you I would enter the convent again because I don't know. Look at the way I am talking! Now as the person who entered in 1939 I possibly would. I would possibly act the very same way. I didn't get much noviceship. I was separated from my friends very young.

It was very fulfilling for me but sad

I got two mortuary cards today. It's sad. The two sisters died before Christmas and then came another, Laurence. She was principal in two of our schools and she did great work and that's for sure. I worked under her and with her for twenty years. I wouldn't agree with everything she did but I had great admiration for her work in the line of education. In the end she got a little loss of memory. When she was laid out I heard some past pupil behind me say, 'She could be in the office', Lord have mercy on her soul. I went down recently to see another sister who is dying of cancer and it was so hard, so sad, to see her there, so beautiful, there so full of life as it were, no sign that she was dying. The two things together, do you know! That's the way it was. This is very difficult.

Am I living now to make up for all the omissions?

Well, there is this point. I think I spoke about visitation and the baby, something that happened when I was a postulant, I think I did. The baby story, I wonder if it is related to the vow of chastity. I was going to leave, but I didn't do it. I don't know what stopped me. But I can say this to you. Looking back on my life now there was many a time I was near leaving and I never did. I never did now. I wonder am I living now to make up for all the omissions?

And it is these things that come up. I didn't leave and there were other times in life that will not come up to me now. Before that when I saw this nun with a little white apron on and I heard about the lay sisters. I was going to become a lay sister to fight for my rights. And I didn't. So I'm telling you these two that come to me now. On the occasion of the baby, where would I go? I was in a town far away, new to me. I had left home. I think I am being too hard on myself. And yet do I not go that far to think about leaving. I belong to the times. I had the conviction but I hadn't, what could you say, the courage to come back, to knock at the door, to know where I was even and say, 'I have to leave'. No, that is a question that I can't answer but I do think of other omissions in my life. They probably turn up in my conversations. What would you call it? It's not altogether a weakness and yet perhaps it is! I leave it at that. I haven't come to grips with it. I had a vocation. Yes, something was calling me. I don't doubt that. But things like that might not upset others. Then my mother was a handy woman, and we would get excited about babies, you know. But I felt strong enough. There was another reason maybe, now why not just say it, say it! Perhaps if I had known there was somebody beside me, or that I could go to, I might have done so. I am this kind. I did not spread it. I did not. Others can talk about things. It went too deeply with me. I didn't have anybody to say it to and I felt I came from something maybe, different yes, totally different. I had come from nature and that deep way of being. I have to leave it at that. Feeling it, having convictions, but yet I did nothing. This is important for me.

I don't feel I could wallop her

I go back to 1964 and I was changed to another convent and the first sickness happened. I got appendicitis and gall bladder at the very same time. The superior was told that Sister Nora was in awful pain and she was out looking at the cattle because the cattle had something wrong with them. And she left me a good few hours waiting and when she came there was nothing she could do but rush me to the local hospital. Now this is interesting. Up to that, we, the nuns, went to the Mater in Dublin. But this was so acute that she had to bring me to the local hospital. She's up in heaven! Then my blood pressure was high. The doctor told me, 'You were on the point of a stroke'. But she left me for three hours. She had to look after the cattle before she came back to me. I had nothing against her. I don't feel I could wallop her. But that was it, the cattle were so important. She didn't tell the sisters that I had a double operation, that I had my acute appendix taken out and also my gall bladder. I still have the stripe. A gall bladder was a big thing because they hadn't the way of today. So she told them then.

It was Easter then and I came home. It was good. I was very good. I came out after a fortnight. There was nobody to take my place in school and I had the Leaving and the Inter Certs, *tuigeann tu*? (Do you understand?). It was near exam time and I had to go back to school in three weeks. Another wouldn't have done it. I wasn't able but I picked myself up and I went on. I was there from 1964 to 1967. That's the year of the Free Education, 1967. I remember saying to the principal who had taught me in school and whom I admired her very much, 'Now I'm in good form and I'm ready for anything you want me to do'.

Sisters, a bit of snobbery

Some superiors were kind and were my friends. Mother Joseph belonged to a very well-off family from Dublin and my poor brother Jim, who is now dead, had ulcers in his tummy and he had a big operation and I wanted to go home to see him. But at that time the sisters used to get the money from home. I'm gone farther back than you can think. You know sisters, a bit of snobbery. Well, maybe I'm wrong in saying that. We'll leave it that way. If they broke their watch somebody at home mended it for them. Oh yes, and anyhow here I am and ordinarily I would write home and ask them to send me the money but I wouldn't. I couldn't. I was teaching and I was better off than my family and poor mother. I put this to Joseph and I told her, 'I'd love to go home but I'm not going because I cannot get the money from home'.

She said, 'I understand fully. You will go home and you won't be sending home for money.'

That stands out for me. What is it, a friend in need? Yes.

Unable to do this job

I came back from retreat to find I was being sent to another convent to start a secondary school. I said to my friend, 'I'm not going to go,' and she said, 'Well if you don't go they'll send somebody else and maybe you have a better outlook', and I burst out crying and I said, 'You're telling me I must go'. I went. I was never interested in administration or running a school. Prior to this I taught and I enjoyed it. We did a little play now and again and I did debates and study. But here I was, having to be a headmistress, talk about being raw. If I was ready to leave when I heard about the little baby, well I certainly felt that I had the worst situation now, that I could not be more unable do this job.

Seventy-eight young girls came to get registered in school. They were gorgeous and they came in, and I was sitting down writing names. So there was free education for secondary schools and the nuns had bought an old rectory, and that was to be the school and the bishop came round. The bishop was the be-all and the end-all at that time. I said, 'Can I get a prefab?' and I got a prefab for £800 and they had it for years and years after I left. So we housed the pupils there. The numbers went up gradually. I was there and the school got on its feet. We got a new school, a secondary school. It's a community school now. Then I was asked to leave. I left.

I gave my blood and I mean that

This time I was summoned to be, not a principal, but vice principal to a man. I said to the Mother General, 'I don't want to take it. I'm not able.' But again I took it. There was going to be a court case over this, 'I won't go to court,' I said. She said, 'You needn't, I'll go'. There were two men who started on the same day. One was made a principal and the other one should have got the other post but she gave it to me. It was mean.

I spent three years there and at the end of that third year I got a brain haemorrhage. I did. It was the hard work. I gave my blood and I mean that. Work was emphasised in my day. Thank God it's de-emphasised, well, not as emphasised today, which is a good thing but I got a brain haemorrhage. It was the Friday before the Leaving Cert and my girls, whom I was very fond of, were there, and I always said, 'You're a team and I'm one of you', and I worked that way. Half way through the class I couldn't get my eyes to move. I thought, do they see there's something wrong with me? They didn't because I got letters from them afterwards and they hadn't noticed. Nobody knew. We were finished and, as I was passing out, the sight stopped. This eye was gone from blood pressure. And I wasn't able for anything else. I got to the end. I was told in Dublin that the clot on my optic nerve was so big that nobody could do anything for me. How could I go through life being blind? I got the grace anyhow. The doctor told me he could do nothing.

I said to the superior, 'Here I am. I'm not able to do anything. I'm not able to put up with life. Go please and do something for me'. She did. And I went to London for a year to learn Braille to learn how to do things for myself as a blind person. At the end I got a diploma. So I came home and there was no place for me now, as a blind person. One day I was sitting alone in the community room and Rose came in and got a book. At the door she said, 'Would you do something about what you did last year'. No more. She closed the door and off she went. I straightened up and I said, 'Bedad, I will now'. I had heard a lot about a school for the blind, I had learned that abroad. I had had further treatment and a wee bit of sight had come back. I would count it a miracle. The doctor would too. So I have limited vision. I can read and I have enough.

I said I would like to teach the blind, if I could. I went to the nun who ran the school in Dublin. I was desperate and, having spoken to me for two hours, she said, 'I'm taking you with open arms'. So I taught with the blind until I retired. Yes, that was nice. And I remember I had a visit from my sister Máirín in England who was a nun whom I admired. She met me and for the first time ever she said, 'I'm proud of you'.

In that now I couldn't be stopped really. Nobody cared for you, that time. Well you had to go, do your own bit. I found a B&B and I stayed there until I left teaching. I loved every minute of it. Others told me when I started teaching the blind that I should never look for thanks. I remember saying, 'That's the least of my trouble'. But the girls were most grateful. When they were getting married I was invited. When they were having their first child I was invited and I am still toing and froing, wonderful friends altogether. And they got on very well but there were no places for the blind at the universities here. And they had to go to England and I still remember the ship leaving Dun Laoire's harbour and I was the only one on the shore seeing five of those girls off to England for third level education. It is memorable.

Máirín, won't you be with me?

My mother on her deathbed said, 'I cannot remember anything and I had the best memory in the parish'. I was there when she died. I was. And that was lovely. I phoned Máirín in England to tell her. I said, 'Máirín, won't you be with me?' She said, 'I'm here and they won't let me home to my mother's funeral'. Sister Patricia was a nurse, and she was long before her time, and she knew that Máirín was upset and she got a photographer in and my mother was there in the brown habit and she looked nice and Patricia had flowers there and the photographer took a photograph that I could send to my sister. How I appreciated that! There are some people and the rules didn't weigh heavy on them. My brother, poor Pat, he's gone and he and not my father gave me money to give to 'that good nun'. Do you see, 'good' nun? And the reason she was so good was that she was before her time.

I said to Máirín at eleven o'clock the other day, 'Máirín, when on earth are you going to send for me?' She died four years ago. She was in the Civil Service and she gave it ten years. She was twenty-seven when she entered. She gave ten years to finish my brother in teacher training, to help all the family. She was wiser than I was. Mine was to go and pray for them. Hers was staying back to help them financially. Well, she had a boyfriend and at the time she left I was at university with all my paraphernalia of a habit. The boyfriend offered her the ring, engagement ring. And she said, 'I won't take it just now because I feel I'm called to somewhere else. But I'd love to marry you. I'll go for a while to see will it suit me to be a nun.' And he said to her, 'I'll wait for you,' and they parted that way. And he gave her two years and she wrote to him in six months and said, 'I think I'm in the right place. Look for another lady.' That's Máirín, who of all the women I have ever met was my idol. Lord have mercy on her.

Some got better chances than others

Changes were coming and they became very obvious in the sixties. But I'm talking about the late forties and fifties. I remember Paula. One first class day and we were talking at our table down here and she was saying, 'I think I'll give up my teaching and learn a course to help the orphans'. She felt that those who were teaching them didn't get a chance. She got a chance of education because she was going to be teaching school. There should have been more care given, that each one would be trained for a job, that's what we were saying. You know, we got better chances than others because we happened to be in schools. They didn't get the same chance, those who were minding the little children. Well, we never spoke about it again. We never did any action anyway. The poor dears, the creatures, when I came they had a white apron on them. What chance did they get? Oh, they would slap. That's for sure. Oh, too much. There wasn't enough of letting out, talking to us, you know, talking about their difficulties. Talk about me not doing things! They wouldn't come up and say, 'It's very hard to mind these girls, we have great difficulty, it's hard to mind these girls' and put their hands to their head and show us how they feel. They couldn't do that. No, no the silence was very holy.

And that slapping happened in the schools as well. I never slapped. But in the primary school, in my time, they slapped. Some were given to the rod. Yes, that's true. But then slapping went on at home and if you told something, told stories out of school, you'd get slapped. Parents wouldn't listen to the whole story. They didn't like you to get into trouble. They were sweeping it under the carpet. I don't think they stopped to have time to sweep it under the carpet. It went in on one ear and out the other.

Abuse came in

There was another mistake. The nuns used to come together and rally to get their favourite in as superior. I believe it still happens. We often say that they didn't pick the finest. There was no change. Abuse came in, then. I listened to the radio last week. The woman on the programme was an orphan and she was in the laundry. Now I never heard worse. She talked on and on, how she became an orphan, how she had a child, how a priest abused her, and how the nuns were awful. And all this and no one spoke, she kept on and on. She said she was going on hunger strike because she only got copies of the letters that her mother used to send her and number two that they were called penitents. The laundry girls were called penitents. She talked about priests and nuns being the worst people. Oh, it was dreadful now. I was going to stop listening but I never did that in my life. I held on to the end. Well, it is very painful to hear it but I think we have to face it. Well, it was the worst I have heard as regards condemning one side totally and no chance to bring out some redemption. When we are listening to this and heartbroken we could go back and ask where did we fail? Yes. This is fair enough to ask ourselves. It's very hard on those who are living, and you can't but carry it. It is only now that these things are coming out. And they are coming out now abundantly.

It's like war. And then the wrong ones get to the top and when money comes into question there are people who need money. Religious have money, this is what they believe and if they have money, get it out of them. Well, that's the game. The broadcaster said, 'We'll put on a bit of music'. He wasn't thinking of the people that were blackened. I don't know how but we have to live through it. Now what brought us on to that? Oh, the fact that in the past we had ideas and good ideas but they hadn't developed to a point where we could group together and challenge. We didn't do it.

Never do that to anybody again

I'm back near home now but it isn't the advantage that people say to me. They're gone, they're gone, there's only one sister alive. Actually, they're building a new convent complex back where I lived for years and if I'm alive when it's finished I'll go back. Would I go back? This place is good enough. I miss the walk to the post office and meeting people. I haven't that now and if I were working I'd be getting to know people and talking to them, now I'm not, and that is huge.

I've written to the provincial team and said, 'Never do that to anybody again'. You know, you're old, your life's work is over, and the friends are made. The history is made. And you're taken out, uprooted out and sent away. Do you know what they did? Once a week one left. These are nuns who were over eighty years of age. I was nearly the last. One person left quietly this week and next week another one. The people were seeing it but it wasn't public. There wasn't any uproar. And the team did it badly, very badly. What did I write to the team? First of all I said I was delighted that the building was going on and I said, 'As a gift, all going well, that I'll be able to go back there'. Something I should often have done in the past. I wouldn't have done it some years ago. You know, yes it's true. I wouldn't be so bold. I took up my pen and I wrote it.

They're re-building now. They could have got a house for us in the town. Earlier I was talking about 1934 and the alienation and you see there's a relationship here. There is. When I went to boarding school I missed all that was going on in the Gaeltacht around home and in the home itself. Now here the superior is grand really. I say that from my heart. But I miss the other. I miss my friends. Six died since I left a year ago. And I went back to each funeral. This morning, I got the sixth mortuary card.

In the past it was the bishop who had too much power but again it wasn't challenged. We obeyed. I could write books about it, just the power they had. He'd come then and we'd be bowing down. He used to look at our books and everything. He did. We were the creatures. Next Sunday the new bishop will be coming and there we will be three hours up at the Cathedral and somebody in this house said, 'We women are just always sitting in the seats'. Women don't have a say except maybe in America. Even to the present day women don't count.

3

Annie

'People started questioning things'

Introduction

Annie is eighty-three years old. She had a privileged upbringing with many extracurricular advantages and she was sent to boarding school in her hometown to give her the best chance possible. Her father was a director of a large business, which he shared with his brothers. They lived in a four-storied house. The family was friends with other business families and the children spent time together. Annie tells some anecdotes from this 'happy childhood' which point to a lack of sophistication and worldliness. Her 'sheltered life' made her an ideal candidate for the indoctrination that was part of the socialisation process in religious life.

Her decision to enter the convent is linked to her memory of being 'mad' at her mother's snide remarks in comparing her to the girl next door who was more socially sophisticated than Annie. She felt rejected by her mother and decided to give herself 'totally' to God, perhaps with the hope that He would be a better mother. But Annie does not join the Carmelites or the convent in England where her mother's youngest sister has recently been received. The priest tells her to join the nuns that she is familiar with and her mother wanted her to stay in Ireland so Annie does as she is told.

Four of Annie's school friends entered with her and the fun happened when the other nuns were at prayers. It is wartime and they have to blacken the windows to be safe from bombs. The blackout is a metaphor for the complete break with the world and the fear she feels when she believes she has to eat everything that is put before her. Her brother's comment that she 'goes to bed with the chickens' is a reflection of how out of kilter with the outside world Annie's life has become. She gives an account of the humdrum routine of life where everyone did everything together, 'filed' from one place to another, where there was a rule for the way a task was carried out, where changing shoes was 'big', where 'running giddily' was forbidden and where to come late merited the punishment of kissing the floor and accusing oneself. This all occurred while observing the blanket ban on speaking to one another. Time was filled with action, leaving no space for reflection, and this defended against the anxiety that reflection and thinking might have brought to the surface.

There was never a space for being creative. At recreation, free time for re-creating oneself involved sewing Sacred Heart badges, answering questions on the previous 'lecture' and eating sweets from 'little dishes' that were carried in on trays. Infantilisation was the order of the day. The convent hierarchy was visible in the refectory. The novices sat at the bottom, the seniors higher up and the superiors at the top table facing down.

Annie's language at times betrays her lack of balance in terms of reality. She maintains a childish perspective. Her uncle is 'mortified' when she carries her 'big win', a jug, around Howth. The Novice Mistress used to 'kill' her when visitors left. She thought 'the world was going to come to an end' when she was transferred but she 'settled down' and 'loved it'. She tells a miraculous tale from the infamous Rodriquez. She continues to use some of the outdated language, such as, she got her 'obedience' which was laced with 'it's God's will' although she knows this is pre-Vatican II speak. It indicates her continued belief in all that happens being the will of God and she believes God was very good to her. She was a child of God.

At every juncture in her life someone told Annie what to do and she never demurred, although she spent a day crying at home after news of a transfer, much to the annoyance of her mother. One could say that Annie represented the 'good nun' and she was rewarded for her docility. She was sent to the US after her mother went to live in California. Later the superior sent her home on a holiday. Another superior at home sent her to the doctor who kept her at home for a year. She got on well with superiors, probably because she never caused them any concern.

Her compliance probably contributed to her illness because life in the US at the time was 'closed in', claustrophobic. Life in Ireland, she muses, was open 'lovely, friendly'. She splits between the two places and projects the good into Ireland. This most likely enabled her to recover.

Reading in the refectory at meals could be daunting and humiliating if one mispronounced words, but Annie cannot attribute those feelings to herself so she projects them into the Novice Mistress who would be 'mortified' if the novice made a mistake. Annie has no way of knowing this to be the case but it encourages her to prepare her reading well so that she is not mortified.

She sometimes manages to be obedient by splitting off her rebellious feelings and projecting them on to others. Brigid, who was older and had been a matron in a hospital, was part of Annie's community. Annie describes her as being 'her own person', 'the boss' who brooked no opposition, although she was not in charge. She rebelled against the system by not conforming and was never punished for it. Annie projected the rebellious parts of herself on to Brigid who did the things she could never dare to do, and while admiring her own split off rebellious parts in Brigid she could continue to be obedient and conformist. But, of course, this left Annie without any way of looking for what she wanted or would have liked to do. Annie says that nuns could become self-centred and selfish which is a bad thing in her mind. To enable her to be happy with her life, she projects all the difficulties on to life outside the convent, leaving her with the better deal.

Annie returned in 2004 to her present convent having spent thirty-six years in the US. She gave her life to God, she did her best with the children she taught and loved. She trusts her God but feels she has not been asked to put that trust to the test. She was obedient and conformist. She had little life experience before she entered and the convent offered her little chance to become a mature adult. She was well cared for in the system and was happy to serve. One is left with a question. Does she feel that she has missed out on something? Has she missed out on not being her own person?

Annie's Story:

I'll treat you all

I must say we had a very happy childhood. There were five children, four girls and a boy. My father had a business. It was a very big business. There were three of them in it and my father was the director. Beside us there was the chemist's family and they were very nice but they were a bit younger than me. But away up the town lived another family of five and we were great friends and the second girl in that family and I were in the same class so every Sunday morning all of us would go for a walk and I can remember a very funny incident.

We didn't have money and my friend found a shilling. We weren't given money going out. We were supposed to go out and not eat anything between meals. We had a good breakfast after coming home from Mass. It was Sunday morning and we'd have a fry and all that. So my friend found the shilling and she said, 'I'll treat you all'. She brought us down to a shop, way down the town, and she told us all to choose whatever we would like and of course being the greedy little thing, I chose a square black bun. As children you would take something you thought you were going to enjoy for a long time. We had all made our choices and we had our stuff and my friend said, 'Now you can pay for them yourselves', and she ran off and we had to leave our goods on the counter and run out after her. She was great fun, always playing jokes and tricks on us.

Every second Sunday evening these friends came down for tea and the next Sunday we went to them. Once we had the concert in what was a pigsty. It was cleaned out. We had another family where there was a talent for music and they joined us and we'd be putting on performances and have great fun. Then when they were down in our house Mom used to always read a story for us all, to keep us quiet I suppose. We'd be playing games, snakes and ladders, draughts and dominoes. So we had really a happy childhood.

A sheltered life

Then when I reached secondary school we went our ways. I was sent to boarding school because they thought that I would work harder, do more. And from there I entered so I had what you'd call a sheltered life really. In my holiday time I'd go to Dublin, up to my aunt and uncle and I had a great time there going out to Bray and Howth and up on Howth Head, and I remember the hurdy gurdies. I loved that. I won a jug and I remember carrying it around and I'd say my uncle was mortified but that was my big win. That time I had no appreciation of all my parents did for us. They did everything. We got music lessons from a very early age. We got elocution. We got every chance.

Funny thing, not long ago I was thinking I used to be mad with my Mom. She would be out next door the night before and I knew well the next morning at my breakfast I'd be hearing about the lovely tray Ellen brought in that night. I always felt it was a rub, you know, and I thought to myself, sure maybe her Mom had it all prepared and she just carried it in. But then after the Leaving Cert I entered.

The Lord was calling me

I felt that the Lord wanted me. I remember very well a day in December 1938 we had Adoration of the Blessed Sacrament. I was in Leaving Cert at the time and I felt very, very strongly that day that the Lord was calling me and I can always remember being very sorry I had to go out to my lunch. I wanted to stay in the chapel. Oh, I have no doubt it was the Lord himself talking to me. And for a while I used to dream about entering in the Carmelites. I thought of giving myself completely and entirely to the Lord and then later I was over at my aunt's reception in London, and they were all saying, 'Come back now won't you in September?' I thought I would. It was lovely. It appealed to me but then we had our retreat and I can always remember the priest at the retreat telling me, 'You'd be better off entering with the sisters you know, that you have been in school with'. And then another point was my Mom didn't want me to go over to London. Mom begged her sister who had just been received into the convent to come back with her. The mistress of novices didn't appeal to Mom and it turned out that she was very good to my aunt and very understanding. My aunt was about twenty-two and she had a boyfriend who was very, very keen and he thought that she might leave and he went over with my grandmother to see her and on the way back he said, 'She'll never come out'. She had everything before she entered. She was the youngest and spoiled and she had a very strong will and was inclined to do her own thing. The Novice Mistress spoiled her, according to my sister who later entered the same order.

World War Two was breaking out

There were six of us, postulants, and five of us had been together in boarding school. It was 1939 and we had the blackout. We'd cover the windows. Everything had to be blackened in case the enemy would see the light and know that people were living there. We had to hang up black on the windows in case they'd drop a bomb on us.

When I went into the refectory the first day I had two poached eggs for my tea. Well, I nearly died and I was afraid but to eat everything. You always had to eat everything that was put before you. The Novice Mistress was very kind. We used to go to bed early. We always had what was called early tea for the first month and we had a great time. When they were all gone down to prayers we'd be having highjinks before we'd go to bed.

It was during the war and petrol wasn't to be got. Now Daddy didn't have a car but my uncles did. Mom got down a few times and they just hired a car to come down for my reception. My brother went home after a visit and said, 'You know the nuns go to bed with the chickens, Annie goes to bed with the chickens'. It was funny.

In religious life, you were treated as a child

Of course, the noviceship then was completely different to the noviceships in later years. It was stricter. It was more like what you'd read about in the old books about religion. The authority was different. In convents, in religious life, you were treated as a child. There was a great respect for the superior and you were kept more as a child.

The call was at twenty to six and you had to be down for Morning Prayer at five to six, and if you were late you did a penance. You had to go out in front of everyone, kiss the floor and say you were sorry for being late. Then we had meditation and we were taught in the noviceship how to meditate. There was a certain formula to follow, the Ignatian model. Then we had office after that. You'd be out at seven. We all filed out.

Our rooms were called cells and we had to do our cell. There were rules for the way you did everything. Then you prepared your bed and all that and you had to be back in the chapel for Mass at seven thirty. Then after Mass we went into breakfast and then we made another visit. We came back to manual work and you had to be sure to be on time for manual work. We all had different jobs around the house, you know, and then we had lecture at five to nine and you always did your sewing. At recreation we used to make the badges and sometimes mother would ask you questions on the lecture. At twenty past nine you had to be on your way to school. You were in school until twelve.

I was sent down to the infant school as a postulant to help out in a class. I was there until twelve. After lunch you went to the chapel and made your examen (daily examination of conscience). At four o'clock we had dinner and then recreation. Weather permitting we went out for recreation and we walked around the grounds. Oh, I should have told you there was silence at every other time. After recreation we changed our shoes again. That was a very important thing. If you wore your house shoes out or if you wore your outdoor shoes in the convent it was a big thing.

We used to read Rodriquez. Well, the big thing about him was that you planted cabbages upside down if the superior told you to do so. He was Spanish priest. He must have lived in a community. His writings were held in high esteem. He demanded great obedience. For example, you don't dot your 'i' or cross your 't' after the first stroke of the bell. He told stories about somebody stitching something and she was an obedient novice and she obeyed the bell and when she came back wasn't her sewing finished for her miraculously! He had a lot of stories like that.

Then at six there was study and the senior in the noviceship was then in charge and you'd have to go up and ask her if you wanted to speak to anyone. You were preparing your schoolwork or learning your Catechism of the Vows and your Holy Rule and your novitiate customs. And there's one of those customs I remember very well: 'the sisters shall not be seen running giddily through the convent'.

At seven we had Matins and after that we had our supper and then it was the wash-up. The novices sat at the lower end of the refectory and the senior community sisters sat higher up and the superiors sat at the top table facing down. The novices did all the serving. Of course, we had reading always at meals except on big feast days. But you had to read and God help you when you were a novice. You had to prepare the reading so the Novice Mistress would not be mortified with you up there mispronouncing words. Supposing there were very few nuns around some night we might be told we could speak at supper. After that we had night recreation until nine. At that time we made those Sacred Heart badges and things like that but we'd have great fun at night recreation. There were thirty novices and we'd have sweets sometimes. The seniors in the noviceship used to put them on little dishes. And we'd dole them out. They'd be all ready before recreation and then we'd carry them in on trays and we'd have them. I remember during retreat time having over eighty nuns in the house.

I forgot about you, Mother

One job I had was to look after Mother Benignus. I had to do her room. She was often in bed. I'd dust and maybe fix the bed. She was meticulous about everything. She had a drawer in her table and she would say, 'Go to my drawer, put in your hand, the left side, down at the corner'. Everything was exactly as she put it and it had to go back that way. And then I had to dry rub her room. Did you know what that was? You had a brush and a pad and you shone the floor. I used to have to get her a glass of water or something and then I had to go back again at three o'clock every day to turn down her bed. She was elderly and had been the superior for a period and she had been Novice Mistress as well. And now I suppose she was in her eighties or nineties. I really don't know but she was old anyway.

One day I was practising because the music exam was coming up and I forgot about her. My God, that was an awful sin! She got a senior community sister to come over and tell the Novice Mistress that the novice hadn't come. So when I went over she asked me what happened and I innocently said, 'I forgot you, Mother'. Well I couldn't have said worse. I forget what happened but I think it died down eventually. Another thing you had to do, if you ever broke anything you had to do the penance or go sometimes to the bursar and she was lovely. And I remember going to her one time and she told me, 'Mother told me to kill you, to scold you'. She didn't scold me.

I'll tell you when I used to get it hard. Although they said the Novice Mistress was nice to me, every time I had a visitor she killed me when the visitor left. I don't know why. I began to notice it was always happening and it didn't take that much out of me, but I did find things hard enough, you know, doing the penance when you came late and that but I didn't find it as hard as others, some found it really hard.

We were received after six months. Then we started the spiritual year and we came out of the spiritual year the following April. Then we went to school as senior white veils. There were six in our group and I had a good friend in a more senior group, who was very good to me. It was during the war and things were rationed, food was rationed but we had a farm and we got healthy food.

They made that choice before they entered

The lay sisters worked on the farm. Maybe out of the eighty sisters there'd hardly be eight lay sisters. They had ceased taking them in my time. Actually the last two were finally professed when I was in the noviceship. I saw very little of them. They were professed sisters and they weren't living in the noviceship. They made the choice to be lay sisters. Oh yes, you had to make the choice before you entered. They mightn't have got as much education as the others. And they weren't able for it after they came. I'm not really sure but I think that was it. I am not sure about dowries. I think the dowries were gone before my time.

I thought the world was going to come to an end

I got my call to training before I had finished in the noviceship and when I came back I was junior community nun and I was teaching in Ireland for the next eighteen years. After some time I got my obedience and I was sent to a very gloomy small town. The convent was small and pokey, a small gate led into it. It hadn't anything very appealing about it really and there weren't many young nuns in it. Oh, I was terribly lonely leaving, because I loved my first convent, loved the school, the children and everything, I was very, very lonely. I thought the world was going to come to an end. It was a complete change and a very difficult change. I settled down and I loved it. I was one of the two juniors there and we did everything but we had a great old time. We enjoyed it. There were only a few of us, about eight altogether.

She wasn't in charge but she was the boss

Brigid, who was a retired nurse, had been a matron in England before she entered and she was a wonderful character. She was herself, she would rule the roost and nobody would say a word to her. This is one funny thing I remember. Brigid's feast day was on the first of February and the second is the feast of the Presentation. Now in the old Holy Rule, the vigil of all these feasts of our Lady were fast days and days of abstinence. So when I went to this convent I found out February the first wasn't a fast day. It was Brigid's feast day. I had to go down to meet the bus to get the flowers that were coming from Dublin for Brigid's feast day. Oh, it was so different. She was a great soul. One of the community nuns had Alzheimer's. She was youngish and Brigid was looking after her. Brigid was a great person. When I was sick she was so good to me. She wasn't in charge but she was the boss. She would look after anyone who was sick. She was an avid reader. There was nothing she hadn't read. The local doctor supplied her with books. She used to visit his house on a Sunday and get a load of them. I suppose she went to the local library too. She was very well up. She was a character and she always talked to herself. You would think there was somebody in the room with her because she would be talking out loud to herself.

At that time you never slept at home

After ten years my next obedience came and I was sent to a big town this time. At that time the ordinary person did not really have a say in electing superiors. It would always be the same people going to the motherhouse from out the country to vote. It was always 'uppeydowney' some used to say. It was in the regime of everything was God's Will. You always got your obedience with,

'Its God's Will that you go to...' It's so long ago now that it's worn off me. That all changed in 1970. When you were transferred after that you would be consulted about it. When you were in the community you were responsible for your own class in school and that kind of thing. I loved the children.

When I got the obedience a friend drove me to my home town because I had a day at home and I never did anything but cry. My Mom now was really tired of me. I was broken hearted. I went to the new convent and from the very day I went into it I loved it. I loved the spirit. Oh, I loved it there. They were lovely. I worked in the school again of course.

My uncle died and he was very close to us, he was my godfather and I was very fond of him. His death was sudden, he had a bad heart. The superior sent word to me that she'd have a bed ready for me in the convent near home. At that time you never slept at home. But the superior general wouldn't let me go up for the Mass, much less stay. That was an awful blow. That was one thing I felt awfully hard. And when she came along on visitation I told her so. But she said, 'Really I couldn't, the rule had just been made before I came into office'. Even Mother Regis couldn't get home to her father's funeral.

They were very strict like that, you hardly ever got home. I did get home one time when my aunt died in 1949. I don't know how I got home that time. Her death was sudden. It was in Dublin. The mistress of novices was going to Dublin on business and she brought me up to see the family. We went on the train.

My Dad passed away

Everything was going grand in my new convent and on Christmas Day, one of the nuns, she was lovely, she called and she said, 'Annie, would you like to go down and see your parents today, to see you Mum and Dad?' I looked at her because before that no one had ever got out of the convent on Christmas Day. Anyway she said, 'There's somebody on her way home and she'll be passing your house, and you could avail of it'. So I took off. I can never forget her kindness because my Mom was very poorly that day and I hadn't heard it or known a thing about it and my Dad was desperately worried about her. A friend came into the house and she said, 'Annie you should not go back, leaving your Mom like that'. So I called the convent and I told the superior and she said, 'Stay there'. I stayed in the local convent at night. There was nobody at home except my Mom and Dad. There are steps up to our house and the kitchen is in the basement. And I remember running down the steps to the kitchen and my Mom, she was so thrilled and excited and she was so poorly at the time. A few days later Daddy was very worried about Mom and he said, 'You go down to the doctor and ask him to come up to her because he sent her to hospital last time she wasn't well and she recovered very quickly'. I was at the convent when I got a phone call from a cousin who said that I should go home, that my Dad was very poorly. 'Oh, not at all,' I said, 'it's my Mom.'

'No, it's your Dad'. It was. They had sent for the doctor. It was a heart attack. So when I got down he was unconscious or very close to it, I don't think he recognised me. He wasn't able to talk anyway and the doctor was very slow about coming and they had to send for another doctor and he was there with them and he said, 'I'll get your Dad into hospital because your Mom isn't able to look after him'. The priest was there too and when the priest came out after anointing Dad and the doctor went in again he said, 'No we can't move him'. And a few friends were there that night saying the Rosary with him. Dad passed away at twenty-five past one. He went peacefully, never even knew it, saying the Rosary.

On Monday morning all the family were home from the US. I couldn't believe it. Mom and I had just finished making the beds and next thing they arrived. Dad had been removed to the chapel. They were home for the funeral but they were not there for the removal the night before. I was the only one there. After the funeral do you know what happened, what people were saying to my mother? They were telling her, 'You should go back to the US with the children'.

'Oh no I couldn't think about it,' she said. When everyone was gone she experienced the empty house. And it's a very big house, our house. There were really four storeys. She said, 'I will go back with the children'. And the house wasn't sold, I mean there was nothing done. She went to California to live with my sister. She stayed and she got on great. But then she came home the following summer to settle things up.

I'm sending you to California

In the meantime didn't I get my obedience to go out to the US! The superior sent for me and I didn't pay any heed. We were always good friends, she had slept opposite me in one convent and we were together in school a lot and I just thought she wanted something and she said, 'I'm sending you to California'. Well, I didn't know whether to laugh or cry or what to do. I was thinking of the house at home and it's very big you know. But things worked out. You wouldn't believe it, before I was due to go wasn't the house sold which was a marvellous thing. Anyway we packed everything in the house. We sent as much as we could to my mother, things that we knew she'd value and that she'd like to have. So that was the end of my time in Ireland. I went to New York. My brother met me and he brought me to his place for a few days. Then he put me on a plane to California to meet Mom. After that I went to my convent.

There was a certain amount of rigidity

The convent was all right but I was only there for one year, then I was six years in the next place. I found it very hard. Even though there was a lovely principal and she was very good to me I have always found it very closed in or something. There were five of us there, struggling, and it was less homely than Ireland. There was more rigidity there. They used to say that superiors who had been in the motherhouse and had never been up the country were stricter. I think our superior was afraid of diverting from the status quo. She and I got on well, very good friends, but on the whole there was a certain amount of rigidity.

I believe that the sisters who started the mission got it very hard because the superiors were so strict. These superiors were very anxious to hold on to the strictness of the rule. I think the American culture had some influence. The Mother General went out on visitation and she was very particular, very, very strict, but I loved her. She's supposed to have told the priest to take up the carpets that they had down in the rooms in one convent. They probably hadn't them in the other places. She was holding on to everything from the Irish motherhouse. She stayed for a year or two and she was very tough on the nuns. She has mellowed out since then but she made it very hard for the nuns in the beginning.

People started questioning things

I went out in 1970. The following year we were all moved. There had been a chapter in Ireland and everything changed. After the chapter some became independent a bit. Before that everyone took everything that was said as Gospel and holy obedience, you know. Now people started questioning things.

That was the year we changed our habits, from the black habit we were allowed to wear white ones in the US and when I arrived they were all making the white habits because they were easier to wash and clean and lighter. It was very hot there. I can remember walking up from school at lunchtime and feeling the sun beating down on me and I thought the convent was too enclosed. You'd get a kind of a phobia. We were closed in, there wasn't space and I'd been in Ireland and things were completely different there. There was a lovely, friendly openness in Ireland.

I didn't get the health. I was working hard that time on my degree too. I used to do it in the summer and I wanted to finish. I was nearly finished. The last course was very hard. We had a very demanding professor and I worked very hard finishing that off with the result that I began to go down physically, and I hadn't intended going home but the regional superior said to me, 'It's time for you to go back to Ireland for a summer holiday'.

So I did and when I came home Mother Patrick saw me and said, 'I'm sending you to a doctor here'. I went to a doctor in Dublin and he put me into the Mater and between the jigs and the reels I had to stay at home. I'd say I was completely run down. I stayed at home and I used to come up and see the doctor and it was going on from month to month in the beginning and then it went to three months and it ended up being for the year.

She was ninety-two when she died

My mother only came home to Ireland once. Instead everyone went out to see her. She said, that wherever your children are that's where you are happy. And it was great for my sister because they had just moved to a new house and you know they had to do the garden and everything and Mom loved gardening. And she was doing the garden and the two little boys were very small and she had a great influence on them, I'd say they loved her. Then later she'd walk them up to school. They were blessed. She was a great help and she was awfully happy there. I remember her eightieth and her ninetieth birthdays. In 1992 she collapsed and she never did very much after that. She got a few months but that was the beginning of the end. She died in 1993. She was ninety-two years old when she died.

I was in the US for thirty-six years

So when I finally went back after my illness I went to a lovely convent. We had a pool and it was really lovely. The librarian had left and the library had fallen into all kinds of disorder. We got it up and running again after a couple of years. I got great help in that library from the lay people around. They were very good to me. The library was attached to the school. It was a lovely school. We got the library on computer and we got it renovated and changed. In all I was nineteen years there. I was in the US for thirty-six years. I came home in 2004. I keep in contact all the time by email and when the four of us are home in the summer we go for a day to Knock.

People outside have a much harder life

I suppose that we really got great chances in the spiritual life. We got some very good retreats, helps in that way. You got time for prayer and you had the Blessed Sacrament in the house.

I really tried to get the best out of the children because I know myself that some people can bring the best out of you and some can bring the worst out of you, and I really tried and asked the Lord for that grace. I was always very conscious of that. I am very grateful to God that the children in my class never had an accident. Before we went out for play I always insisted on saying the prayer to the Guardian Angel. I'd say that God was good to me.

In the past some felt that a sister mightn't have been fair or that she had an edge on you for some reason or another. Sometimes it was because someone else was very nice to you or gave you notice. I heard of that but I didn't experience it. As a teacher I'm sure I made plenty of mistakes but I would definitely do it all again. I wouldn't change that. People outside have a much harder life. I would say too that we could get very self-centred, selfish. I think it was a great thing when we were allowed to go home and we could see that people at home had a lot more to put up with. It took us out of our comfort zone. It was good to be in school to see what parents had to put up with. I wondered how on earth they could keep up with all the demands on them in the Catholic school, in the US that is. They were paying fees and everything else. Even though they're young and maybe in good jobs the parents have to work mighty hard. I think the world is much harder now.

I take things as God's Will

I find personally, but it's my own make up, that I take things as God's Will and I found out that it always works out for the best. I trust God that he'll always do what's best for me. I have a firm conviction of that. I trust God. I think I do but you know if I were put to the test I might not be that cocksure of myself. That's the honest truth. Thank God I was very happy everywhere I went.

4

Birdie

'We weren't prepared for life'

Introduction

Birdie is eighty-five years old and she looks back at her life with anger and sadness. Her parents owned a business in a large country town and she often helped there, which gave her a business sense that was never acknowledged or fostered in the convent. She is forthright in condemning the wrongs of religious life and honest about her rebellion and defiance of authority. She rather revels in being 'disobedient', and probably feels she has nothing to lose at her age and has an opportunity of letting the world know what it was really like, at least from her perspective. The others, who are 'too correct' to misbehave and have a deep faith, are unlike her as she is full of doubts.

Her experience of the death of her four siblings as infants left her with a terrifying fear of death, which has remained with her all her life. Such was her fear that when, at eighteen years of age, she was wheeling her baby sister in her pram and she cried Birdie thought the baby was going to die. The ever-abiding feeling of cold is indeed real in the poorly heated convent, but it is also a metaphor for the lack of comfort, companionship and love.

Her sister Sarah died of TB as a young adult and Birdie wishes she had been 'diagnosed on time', but resigns herself to the fact that there was 'precious little cure' for it anyway. What other timely diagnosis does she wish had come to pass? As a teenager she spent time with the 'fellas' around town and her parents were 'worried' so they sent her to boarding school. How wild was she?

She tells her mother she would never have entered the convent if she had not sent her away. Her mother is standing at the range at the time, a metaphor for the warmth of love which has been denied Birdie. Is she saying that if her mother had kept her in the family and allowed her to continue socialising with boys she would have married and been happy, but that she did not 'diagnose' that 'on time' and now there is 'precious little' can be done to remedy it? She was seduced, not by boys, but by God and the Church's promise of heaven which she no longer believes anyway. God was drawing her in and she longs for a transcendent experience but it does not fully satisfy her. She is drawn to 'sacrifice' and she chose the cold convent instead of a warm relationship and a range of her own to permeate heat throughout her life and her house.

This 'loose thing' from her unconscious that she immediately recants is the rage she feels at her mother and the sadness she has endured as she battled her way through loneliness for 'a man' and succeeded in living without deep love. She feels the rage at the sexual repression demanded by life in the convent. She rages at the demand for blind obedience, the godly status of the superiors, the way they held on to power, the way they exploited her parents financially and the fact that they never allowed her to grow up and 'mature'. She is deeply resentful of the favouritism and cossetting of her companion by those in charge. Birdie was forced to sit at the 'vegetable table' (the naughty corner) for her meals for a week because this companion complained that she had 'brushed against her white veil'. No one dared speak out about injustice; everyone feared for her own well-being and sanity; she might be the next victim.

Besides the repressed rage there was a constant unrelenting fear in the past. Birdie was afraid of her father at home and she transferred that fear to the superiors in the convent. She can feel the rage; it makes her 'blood boil'. The fear and rage and repressed sexuality are heartbreaking, and because they were not fully acknowledged and worked through Birdie got a 'heart attack'. She would have liked to attack those who held too much sway in her life but she somatised her emotions and the attack was directed inward to her heart, the seat of love. Like many of the nuns her love found expression in her teaching and her contact with pupils, which offered some respite from the monotonous, unnecessary scrubbing and polishing and emotional turmoil of the convent. She argues to and fro, from distressing feelings to feelings of peace, from unhappiness to happiness. She dare not come down on the side of unhappiness so she continues to waver.

Her parents uprooted her from the 'gay' life she had at home and this experience is repeated when she is moved in her retirement to a house where she did not feel welcome in spite of her pleas to be sent to a house where her companions lived. Later she moved again, this time to her companions who share an 'ordinary' life with her. But her relationship with them must remain on a superficial level. Perhaps she feels that this exploration of the past has gone far enough. She does not want to delve any deeper; it would do 'more harm than good'. Perhaps she is worried that she has revealed too much already and that she must somehow preserve some hope for the 'half normal' side of her that she has managed to salvage from the storm of early convent life. If she did not have her walking stick she would fall. She must prop herself up for the days ahead as she 'just battles away'.

In the convent Birdie acted out by doing her own will, in as far as this was possible. She repressed her sexual feelings and her rage but the result of this was that she lived in extreme fear. She paid a high emotional price for not conforming, but she enjoyed the excitement of being a rebel.

Birdie's Story:

I met with death early in life

Three boys died. They all died of pneumonia. Then I had a little sister who was killed in an accident. Poor Sarah was twenty-one when she died; she had just begun nursing. She was coming home on the bus and got a terrible wetting and a dreadful pain in her side, and the doctors thought it was appendicitis but actually it was pleurisy and developed into TB. If only they had diagnosed her on time! But there was precious little cure for TB! She was a fine girl, she was lovely, the only one of us that was a fine girl. She was the second youngest. Eileen was the youngest, eighteen years younger than me. We were very close. I can remember wheeling her out in the pram and she started to cry and I started to cry with her because I thought she was going to die. And when I came home my poor mother was shocked because she thought something had happened. I shouted, 'Mammy, she's crying, she's crying!' Mammy only laughed at me then.

I attended my local secondary school until the final year. Then I was sent to boarding school. I was having a great time, out walking around the town and fellas and everything and my parents were probably worried about me and the best thing was to take me off the streets. It was an awful mistake; you know, I was at a terrible disadvantage to change school in sixth year! If my parents had known anything about education they'd never have done it. I only scraped the old Leaving Cert and then when I was a postulant I did it again.

Poor Sarah was sent to boarding school as a first year. It was terrible, dreadful! Looking back I can remember her, at study, crying away and that used to break my heart and I tried to keep up for her. I remember saying to my mother at the range, 'Mammy, I'll never forgive you for sending me to boarding school'. If I hadn't been I wouldn't have entered because I was having a good time at home. Even with all the restrictions at home I had a certain amount of freedom. School and convent were much the same, yes, much the same, but I certainly would never have entered had I not been taken away from the gay life that I had at home. I never regretted entering, no matter what I went through. I was always basically happy so that's a loose thing now that came in. There was something there, calling me. I don't know what you'd call it but there was something there and then I'd try to forget about it. Then one of the nuns approached me and asked me if I'd like to enter the convent and I remember saying to myself, Oh, my God, no!

Silence all day and a coldness between people

I'll talk about religious life when I entered in 1940. Now, of course, everything was very severe and we accepted it because we came in for a life of sacrifice. You got up early in the morning. The only place there was a bit of heat was in the chapel and you were sleepy, you went to the chapel and you were dead sleepy. You were warm enough in the chapel but anywhere else in the house the cold was terrible, terrible. Now you would be up about half past five and if you were on the call you were up earlier. Then you had to take your turn at the furnace, poking it and making sure it kindled and often enough it would go out. And there'd be murder if the heat didn't come on in the chapel.

We had the Office, meditation, Mass and then we had break-fast in silence. Now the food was scarce, very plain but of course that is what people were used to at that time. You'd get enough bread and we ate it until it nearly came out our eyes. Then you had silence all day and you'd meet a companion and you just looked at her, which was very queer. The great emphasis was to keep you working. We washed floors and we were all the time polishing and dusting. The whole thing was a stress on manual work, sure we killed ourselves waxing and polishing and nothing in the way of books that would educate us. No way could we read anything. I don't know how we escaped at all, how we're half normal. I sup-pose life on the whole was very simple for people except for those who had money. I say all this was no help to maturing. I'd say it was to knock any bit of spirit out of us and to keep us occupied. It wouldn't do for us to have nothing to do; to be idle would be very bad for us. Now, it wasn't that they needed us to clean the house because there were more than enough nuns. If we weren't at our prayers we were polishing or dusting.

The light was put out at ten o'clock at night. We never had a drop of hot water to wash with and we didn't get a bath until first profession, two and a half years after entering. We only had cold water and I used to be awake half the night with the cold and then we used to be hungry as well. But the thing that I felt most was the cold, the awful cold. To this day I have a fear of the cold. There was no homeliness in the big convent. Nothing homely. It was cold, nothing familiar. Back in those times there was a cold-ness between people.

You got some kind of a light supper at night but it wasn't any good. It was leftovers from earlier. One time, if you were sick you got an egg for your supper. And I had been very sick and by mis-take I had been given an egg and the superior sent the server to take the egg from me. Wasn't it dreadful? Yes, that the truth. Yes, take the egg from you! It was wartime and you had rationing. I used to spare my sugar and when it would come to the end I had nearly half a jar. I was sparing it so much to make sure I'd have it. Each one got her little jar of sugar, her own ration of sugar. The boarders had the same as us. You got dessert on a Friday. On Sunday you got some dessert or other and for supper, as we called it, you got porridge. Raphael and I were on study in the boarding school and she used to be so hungry that she'd eat too much porridge and she'd get sick, dead sick. Oh yeah, butter. You got the smallest little bit to last you, I don't know if it was for the week or the month but it was very small. You had to keep it in your place in the refectory.

It was dreadfully unfair

There was lots of unfairness. Raphael went to train as a nurse in England, as a white veil, before profession, and the war broke out and she had to come home. She was treated with kid gloves. She was on a pedestal because her family was important in the town. She was always grander than us and she didn't have to comply with any of the regulations. One day I passed her and brushed against her white veil and she complained and the superior told the poor Novice Mistress to put me sitting at the vegetable table in the refectory for all my meals for a week. That's the truth and the superior passed me one day, oh, it was awful, and she said, 'Who put you there, dear?' And she had done it herself! Everyone would be afraid to talk about it. Afraid, yes, that's right. Afraid and even though they'd know it was dreadfully unfair and everything there'd never be a word said.

We had to hand up any gifts we got. I remember getting toothpaste and soap and sewing material, needles and thread and all these things. All taken up from me but the hard part was they were often given to someone else who was in favour.

Then life was very regimented. At first recreation we sat down and we sewed or did knitting. Second recreation was much the same, monotonous was the word I was trying to think of there. I don't know how we got through it. I still think of Sunday evenings and I have a dread of them but it was the same every evening. On a Sunday afternoon, one-thirty to four, we sat in the community room at study, correcting copies, oh, it was terrible, awful now. And then I think how did we manage at all? On first Sunday oh you were in deep silence all day and we used to have an interior examen at one-thirty, and the first question was: Am I ready to die? I never got past that one, never. I sat wondering was I? Was I?

Well my companions were young with me and we were gay and good-humoured and we laughed at things instead of sitting down and crying at them. The life didn't help to mature us. They were out to make us docile and dependent. Once the Novice Mistress went to Dublin and she brought back the song 'Lord for Tomorrow'. She brought it back to me to teach me to do the Lord's will and to obey because I was very self-willed.

None of the superiors had any sympathy for you if you were sick. I remember being in terrible pain, with periods, and you had to keep going and you would be polishing floors and you wouldn't even get a drink to help you. You wouldn't be allowed go to bed. You had to stay on your feet and you had to be up at half five the next morning. Oh, it was very hard.

I got inflammation of the womb and I was very ill and the doctor came in. I was only in my twenties. There was TB in our family. He said, 'That little nun is in great pain,' and he said I should be sent to the nearest hospital, but Mother Regina wouldn't let me go. He thought I should have a hysterectomy. Mother Regina sent me to Dublin. I was sixteen weeks in hospital on, now I can't think of the drug, it's not used now but it cured me. I had injections three times a day, if not more. Then the tablets – big, black tablets – and I couldn't take them and they had to give them to me in liquid form. But this is the bit I wanted to tell you about that. Brigid, a community nun who watched everything and reported to the superiors, was worrying about the superiors having to pay for me in hospital, and what did she do? She thought it would be better for my parents to pay for me, that the community wouldn't be able to do it, they'd have to get rid of me. She got my sister to tell my parents to pay for me. My parents didn't tell me, they didn't want to worry me when I was so sick. You see, I was very delicate.

Now later another nun came and she was very delicate but then you had a different regime. The superiors were better to her. I suppose they felt her parents wouldn't have money but my parents had it. By golly, if they did the nuns took anything they could get from them. Then they had to pay for me in the novitiate, apart from the dowry, for my training in the novitiate. There was a fee every three months. Now I doubt if others had to pay that. It was just because they felt that my parents had money. They drained everything they could out of them. So much so there was very little left for my siblings. That's a fact. You know, it annoys me when it comes up. Trying to forget about it is best. I don't let my sisters give me anything to make up to them.

And as for spirituality you didn't get a whole lot. I remember for spiritual year we had Rodriquez, oh Lord, such stupid old stuff, and we'd be hoping when the book would be finished we'd have something else, ah no, back with Rodriquez again. That's all we got the whole spiritual year. And particularly in the spiritual year you did nothing only polishing. We got no education in Scripture, nothing, Old Testament, New Testament, Liturgy nothing. I can remember a young nun mentioning Psalm 50 – my God, I knew nothing at all about it!

I was sent to teach

Then you were never asked what you would like to do, nursing or teaching or anything else, you were just sent to something. I was sent to university. As I told you my sister, Sarah, died when she was only twenty. I wasn't let visit her in hospital or anything and I was under terrible strain when I went back after her funeral. Then my health broke down, I was delicate anyway. I went back then it broke down again and they said the second time it was a nervous breakdown, slight but it was there. So that was the end of the university. I was sent to teach without further training.

School and supervision of study were a great escape for us. It was great to get away from the discipline and confinement. I loved the pupils. They were not like they are nowadays. They were grand. They were lovely. I was very happy. But you were watched all the time because you daren't speak to them and I used to see the boarders to bed at night and I'd talk away to them. You weren't supposed to. It was awfully funny; you couldn't speak to them then but later on when things loosened out a bit they were mad for us to talk to the girls. I'm saying that getting up to the boarding school was another relief from all that dreadful life that we had.

Then the letters we sent out were read and the letters we got in were read. I got a letter from a past pupil and she was telling me about this friendship and she said that it was a platonic friendship and the superior opened the letter, of course. Well she didn't know the meaning of platonic; she thought it was something terrible. She said that I wasn't to write to this girl any more. Somehow I got a letter out to her to tell her to mind what she was writing to me and the next letter she wrote a big plaster 'private' on it to get me into more trouble, good God!

We'd put white hankies on our heads

You see we were never let out on walks or anything and going back from holidays it was like going back to a prison. And I remember Antonia and I used to steal out for walks, in the dark, and we'd put white hankies on our heads. We put them over the veils so that the traffic, whatever traffic there was, horses and carts, would see us. We were terrified. You see, I'd never have been what you'd call 'a good nun', an obedient nun. One night we went down the town and the doctor's house was up for sale and Antonia said,

'Sure I was never at an auction in my life.'

'Neither was I.'

'Come on, let's go in.'

'No, if anyone sees us we'll be killed.'

'Okay, if you won't go I'm going.'

'All right, I'm going home.'

But she changed her mind and came home. We were at our supper and news came in that the floor had gone down on all who were in the auction and they were all brought to hospital. Talk about a miraculous escape. Jesus, Mary and Joseph if it had come out that there were two nuns in the catastrophe and we not supposed to be outside the door at all. Oh good God!

What did the canon want with you?

Then small breaches of discipline, like breaking silence, especially the great silence at night, was greatly exaggerated, you'd nearly think it was a mortal sin. And then another one, if we met a priest in the garden we had to report that we met him and not alone that, we were supposed to tell the conversation we had with him, which, of course, I never did anyway. I'd say a lot of us didn't.

A couple of times the canon asked me to do things. He'd be walking round the garden and the superior would be below at the other part of the garden watching and I would go anywhere in the garden to avoid him because I knew she was watching. He was looking for me because he wanted typing of a very confidential nature done. Anyway, she got me and she said, 'What did the canon want with you?' I said, 'Mother it was confidential'. That nailed my coffin altogether. Nailed it. Twice that happened to me. She gave me a dog's life. She was terrible to me, terrible.

Teresa was sacristan and she was talking to Father Martin in the sacristy and they took her out of her job and they put her out to mind Stella. That was her charge, to mind Stella, the old dog. Father Martin used to die laughing over that. You see, Teresa would chance her arm and talk to the priest.

He was affectionate with me

Friendships were looked down upon. Oh the loneliness of it! The hardest thing in my religious life was loneliness. Now it wasn't loneliness for my parents or my home. It was loneliness for a man. That's what it was. I want to tell you that. Then to make it harder you weren't allowed friendships at all. You know, they were totally condemned! Well, you fought the battle of being able to do without friendship. You just fought the battle and you were delighted when you fought it and were able to carry on without friendship. For me, it would have been a conquest that I was able to go through life and not feel that awful need of friendship and someone to love deeply.

I was very great with Father Brian and he was very fond of me. And you know it was at a time when you couldn't talk to anyone. I was sick in the infirmary and he'd steal up to me. Jesus, Mary and Joseph, when the nuns were at their breakfast he'd steal up to me! I suppose I was twenty-four or so. He was young too but he wasn't as young as I was. He was probably thirty. I didn't feel any guilt about it. You know, he was affectionate with me, just a kiss or a hug and that was it. I wasn't the type to have scruples about things. And then he left. I had to go through all that suffering on my own and no one knowing about it. I was so lonely and I swore to God that never again would I get involved with anybody. He was gone and I had to paddle my own canoe, and eventually, when I was able to do that, I was delighted with myself. Oh yes, a big loss and that, I suppose, was the hardest separation for me. I'll never forget that. To think that I could go ahead now and get over that, that was the hardest battle for me.

The canon was crazy about Antonia. She would go up to school and the canon would be up there. I remember something about the canon lifting her over the wall. Evidently the terrace door was locked and she couldn't get back into the convent and he helped her to get over the wall. Yes, that's what made life kind of juicy for us. We did our own little things, only not to be caught. That was important. But there were people who would be too correct to behave that way. A lot depended on the type of people that you lived with. Now, there were some beautiful people and there were some troublemakers. I hated Catherine. Yes, she was horrible, rough and nasty. Leave it to Brigid; she was terrible. She was very immature. She was a trained teacher when she entered but she was dreadfully immature.

These children had nobody to stand up for them

Brigid watched us all the time and brought stories down then to the superiors. And if she didn't see anything, she got information from the industrial school children who were up in school. You know, they were talkative children. I had a class and they were doing shorthand and a young girl asked me would I like to go on the missions and I said 'no'. She went back to Brigid who put a different construction on it and told the superior. I was sent for and the superior was very unjust with me over it. Now I was leaving over that. I said, 'I'm not staying with injustice'. And the only one I told was my companion and she said, 'Birdie, wait for a while, don't act on impulse'. And I stayed. I said, 'Well I came for God and I'll stay for God'.

Brigid would slap these children. She was cruel. Brendan would do it too. She was in charge and she was horrible to these children. She was a bully. They talk about the great things she did in the industrial school and I always say she could do what she liked. Rose worked there. She was my friend and she would tell me. She used to be raging. One time she would be getting on great with Brendan and the next time there would be murder. You see, Rose would play up to her, I suppose to survive. Rose knew what was going on because a few times she came very upset to me because of the beating Brendan gave the lads. She often came down to me in a terrible state, shocking state. If you faced Brendan she was down to report you to the authorities. One nun faced up to her about her bullying tactics and Brendan couldn't stand her and anyone she disliked she got rid of. Of course, the superiors knew. It was accepted. These children had nobody to stand up for them.

It makes my blood boil to think of it

I wouldn't want to go back in time. I wouldn't be able for the early life that we had. God, I'd go mad to be regimented all day long. I couldn't take it at all. You were watched and if superiors took to you you were all right but if they were against you it was too bad for you. They watched everything you did and put constructions on things, most unjust. They were suspicious of everything. You were forbidden to do this and do that and meet people and be natural with them. The whole thing was protecting you instead of letting you face dangers and see how you coped with them. Wasn't it terrible that we lived in fear? You were in a little shell. You couldn't oppose them. You see, there was fear, terrible fear. It's just that they had so much power, and their word was law, and you daren't oppose them, and oh God, you couldn't. I really don't know but there was terrible fear. It makes my blood boil now to think about it. We behaved very childlike and very immature and that's wholly all of it. Now what comes into my head is that they had no respect for us, and no real care for us, and that was sad because we were so precious to our parents who made sacrifices for us and then to come in and be treated like dirt! The only important people were those who were intellectually brilliant, and even they wouldn't be nice to them because they would be a threat to them, they'd become too cocky. They wouldn't put anyone into positions of authority that would question them.

When Paul and Patricia were superiors we were getting bolder. It was a bit like that in homes too. You see, in my home it would have been my father I was afraid of, not my mother. Women, the creatures, didn't have many rights, no, they didn't. You would think that is surprising because you don't understand the mentality of people in those times. You were just a subject and that's it and you didn't question it. You see, we didn't question anything. Life was very tough under Paul and Patricia, and it was time to get rid of them. Three nuns used to come up to talk to me in the basement in the boarding school (I slept in the boarding school looking after the boarders) and to ask me to vote for two others and to get rid of Patricia and Paul.

Then one day I was sent to the office and Patricia and Paul were there and said that they heard what was going on and asked me if I had anything to tell them, and I said no and I didn't tell them and I wouldn't tell them what was going on. I was coming down the stairs and I met my companion and I said, 'They'll be sending for you and they'll be asking what you know'. I discovered later that she had been there before me and had told them everything. So that'll give you an idea. My co-conspirators were then shipped off to the missions. They would have shipped me too but my father was very good to them, in the way of giving them coal and tea and sugar and things in the war years so they didn't send me. One day the superior said to me, 'I'd have sent you on the missions only your father asked for you not to go'.

I had great peace no matter how hard things were

Community life is the most difficult part of religious life, definitely, and I suppose that's why people are going to live in apartments. I had great peace no matter how hard things were. Now it is different, very different, but in spite of this I could never say I was basically unhappy; if I were, I would have left. There must have been some grace there, there had to be, because I was the type of person who would enjoy life and friendship and everything. Yet strangely enough, I can't explain it, but there was a basic happiness there all the time. There was always something, God seemed to be always drawing me to him. There's something there that draws me. It's not that I'm comfortable in religious life that I stay. There is something between God and me, there is something there, something pulling me. I mean, when I was younger I could have walked out and done something else. But something stopped me, there's a draw all the time. I wasn't afraid of leaving. No, no that was never the case. I'd have too much character for that. I've great courage and I'm a devil when it comes to courage, even if it's only expressing my opinion. I don't give a hoot what anyone thinks of me. No, I don't care. There's a draw that I cannot explain and deep down I was always very happy, very content, which is something I should thank God for.

That was the first bit of freedom

Then as time went on life got easier, and you didn't care, you got out for walks and then we had a free half day, once a month, and sure that was gold to us. And we used to bring picnics and go out, to some hill or somewhere and we'd sit there and have our tea.

It was marvellous. You'd only get bread and butter. That was the first bit of freedom. And then by degrees we were allowed home and you could go out if people invited you out, out for tea, but then people wouldn't have known that we could go so we didn't get out much.

Then, I forget the date, at the end of the Chapter, the Mother General visited us and she lambasted us over everything, the way we were behaving, everything was wrong with us and the convent was in very poor condition and we had asked for it to be renovated and she said, 'You're looking for something to be done to the convent but I'm telling you nothing will be done with it, nothing'. Oh she read us and she didn't wait for her tea, she couldn't after the abuse she had given us. Had she done something at that time she could have saved us going out into small houses but we won't call them small. I had to move to one. It was the hardest thing because the group had already settled in and I suppose I was intruding on them if you like. I didn't feel wanted. I was an outsider, always an outsider, and the nun in charge was very nasty to me, very ugly to me.

I nearly died with the cold

I remember they all went to school except myself and the heat was turned off at half nine. I nearly died with the cold. I had retired and it was the depths of winter. I went out in the morning for something and I met a past pupil. 'God,' she said, 'isn't it dreadfully cold. I'm going home to the fire.' I said, 'It's well for you having a fire to go to'. I can always remember that. I'd no heat and later on referring to being so cold in that house someone said, 'Why don't you put on your heater?' and another said, 'That's very expensive,' meaning I wasn't to put it on. I thought of that, this morning.

I wouldn't go to the community room at night. I went to my room; I felt that much left out. I remember waking in the morning and I hated facing the day. Hated it, but would I have left? No, that something that was there but I hated facing my day for a long time, quite a few months. Then gradually I felt at home and I settled down. I had a massive heart attack and I often thought that it was the stress, but I think there was a lot of cholesterol in my blood. I don't know, maybe it was the stress in this house. I had been pulled away from everyone I knew all my life. I begged the Mother General to let me come here to this house with the group I knew because I was at home with them. She couldn't because there was no room so I had to battle that. I can never honestly say that I was at home in the other house.

We weren't prepared for life

I'm very strong on this: we weren't prepared for life, especially life as it is now. We had no training in cookery. We weren't allowed into the kitchen and we had no experience of cooking and, as I said, that is a terrible drawback today where there are five or six of us. We got no training whatsoever in the kitchen. You had to get permission to go into it and that's affecting us now, a bit late for me. You see, my parents had a business and if you were helping at all it was in the business. So therefore when it came later on and we went into houses and we had to cook, oh, the Lord God, it was a nightmare, a nightmare, and I have met several nuns since who say the very same thing, scared out of their wits.

We never travelled and I can remember being driven to Dublin. I think Antonia was in hospital. Sure I hadn't a clue where we were. I had never been in Dublin, ever. So that was another drawback. The small houses, it's demanding you know. If we could get out and have our cars and be totally independent but sure at my age there's no point in it at all. Sure, it's grand in that you have your independence but you're working very close to people, which is very demanding. So then to talk to you about life as it is now. Coming out here was another change. I knew them all so well but living with people is a different thing. I often look around and say this is lovely house.

Life is very homely here

But our house was so cold last night. Well, I feel the cold. I felt so cold this morning. I said to myself why is it so different to an ordinary house? Well, an ordinary house would have a range in the kitchen and the range would give heat to the whole house and give a warm atmosphere and you'd have somewhere warm to pop into, whereas we had no heat. The house here is too big. It's worse in summertime because all the heat goes off. I have a blocked valve in my heart. My head is just grand now but it gets so light and if I didn't bring a walking stick with me I'd fall. Yesterday it was bad. I had a bad old day with it. But the doctors can't do anything for me. There's nothing that can be done except put up with it.

Life is very homely here. You just behave in a very ordinary way with people. You've no put on or anything. Then, of course, at any time you're not going to talk at a deep level. I just don't want that and I don't need it now, no, I don't, thanks be to God. I talk and give out my opinion in a very ordinary way, which is nice, but for talking in a deep way about myself I wouldn't be on for doing it. I don't want to do it, and I suppose I don't want to delve into myself either. It would do me more harm than good.

I still visit people; the need is there to let them talk about their troubles. They have confidence in the nun. Some of them I have known a long time but there are new people that crop up. People would say to me, 'Come down to see me will you?' But I couldn't keep up with people. I wouldn't be able to keep up with all who ask me and I feel very guilty about that. I'm just not able. Social services are giving them material help but they want someone to sit down and listen to their troubles.

I find faith very difficult

I wouldn't say that my faith would ever have been strong. I used to envy the ones whose their faith seemed so deep; mine was shallow. I listen to lots of radio programmes; they are very god-less and they're critical of the Church and its bound to rub off on me. I find faith very difficult. I just battle away. Life hereafter, God, I don't think I believe that at all, that's the truth. I don't really. Sometimes people say to me, 'People die and they never come back', and it puts that question in my mind. Some of the nuns' religion is all superstition, this saint and that saint and holy pictures. I've no time for that kind of religion at all. There's very little difference between our life and the people who are not in religious life. They are making far more sacrifices than we are. I think they should let religious life go.

5

Mary

'Most of the nuns were not trained for the work'

Introduction

Mary is now eighty years of age. She had an early separation from her parents and siblings. She stayed with her grandparents for a few years when her father was transferred and the family moved away. Nobody ever spoke to her about this. She supposes it was because there were so many children younger than her to be looked after. When she returned to her parents she continued her education in a primary and secondary school run by nuns.

In the mid-1940s prospects for the young were not very bright in Mary's local town and many had to move away for further education and for work. Often it was the men who emigrated and the women who remained at home dependent on money they received from England. Entering the convent was a way of attaining security. Three of her aunts had become nuns and Mary and her siblings followed in their footsteps. She and her three sisters became nuns in Ireland and her two brothers became Christian Brothers. One brother found the life was not for him so he left and married.

There is some evidence that Mary's early break in her attachment pattern may have left her with some residual unconscious rage that influenced her decision to want to leave mother and go to China to become a nun. In this decision, Mary is rejecting her mother's life in favour of the fantasy of an exotic life in China. However, a priest talked her out of it. She suspects the nuns colluded with the priest about this. She conformed to the priest's wishes, like a 'good girl' who bows to superior male authority. Mary is not in touch with her anger about this and uses her siblings as a way of expressing it. They were, she believes, coerced into becoming nuns. Does she feel now, in retrospect, that she too was coerced but feels it would be too dangerous to express this? Her recent feelings of abandonment by the leadership team after years of diligent and assiduous service to the order may have coloured her perspective on her initial response to her vocation.

Mary was accepted in her local convent although there was a policy to send local girls to other convents. This was to enable them to make a complete break with the world, severing links with family and friends, which served to intensify the bond with the community. It reinforced the convent ideology that precluded doubt and uncertainty, and offered eternal salvation, and even sainthood, as a reward for fidelity and perseverance. The sisters inevitably lost contact with changes in society and this left them somewhat anachronistic and increased the difficulty when they, later, tried to fit into the contemporary world.

Mary wore her mother's wedding dress at reception, reinforcing the separation from her mother's life, being mother, and not being mother. She was professed in 1949 and in 1969 she was elected as local superior because a convent needed to be renovated to adapt to the changing times. This was the beginning of an eighteen-year period in leadership, a merry-go-round of activity that Mary seemed to enjoy.

At the first diocesan chapter in 1972 Mary was elected as Mother General. Father James, as advisor to the chapter, had no authority but Mary ceded her authority to him, much in the same way as she obeyed all authority, unquestioningly and mindlessly, because, in the Church, all men were deemed to be authorities. This lessened Mary's sense of agency and made Father James more important. At his instigation she began her rounds of visiting in Ireland and the US and appointing leaders and principals in most of the convents.

When the team was appointed at the first chapter they were offered accommodation in a convent with a Magdalen laundry attached to it. They accepted the offer without inspecting the premises. This showed they had much to learn about human nature because the premises were entirely unsuitable and allowed the sisters who resided there the opportunity to resist the changes that were taking place. They could vet those who came to see the team and could overhear conversations through the thin walls. Soon the team found more suitable accommodation.

As Mother General, Mary had a Magdalen laundry and a residential childcare home under her jurisdiction. She thinks the women in the laundry have 'strange' stories. She immediately sets them apart as different. She is aware that there is some criticism of her institutions, of mothers and children not being permitted to see one another. She denies this, but thinks it could have happened. Her confusion about the truth of the matter could be a way of denying the feelings of anxiety and distress that the women must have suffered in being deprived of their babies. And, of course, when Mary was a little girl she may not have seen her own mother for some years when she lived far away with her grandparents. All feelings have to be split off.

Mary gives some insight into the morning schedule in the Magdalen home, namely, being called by the nun, sleeping in dormitories, washing side by side, collective morning prayer, Mass, collective thanksgiving, breakfast and then off to work. She is conflicted in her view of the nun in charge. She says she was 'caring' and follows this with the revelation that she even inspired fear in the nuns. The women worked without pay as did the nuns who worked in the laundry. The nuns were uneducated. They were probably lay sisters and many of the women could not read or write. Mary believes they should have been taught but then she withdraws from her criticism of the order by saying that many of them were slow, implying they couldn't be taught in any case. Then she is unsure and wonders if they were always like that or if it was a result of their life experiences. She is grudgingly open to the possibility that all of these women may not have been lacking in intelligence, but that the lifestyle imposed on them may have been detrimental to their developing personalities, but she cannot stay with the thought and immediately adds that she does not know. She was in charge and she did nothing. Her meandering suggests she may be trying to repress her guilt. Each time Mary begins to reflect she retreats and takes another course. Both the nuns in the laundry and the women there were without education, while the order educated poor, intelligent girls gratis by awarding them scholarships to secondary school. One can only suppose that this was not accidental. The system had to be maintained. Some people had to be kept in their place, a place of servility and slavery.

Mary goes on to say that the Magdalens were some kind of secular order, 'semi-sisters'. It is believed that the nuns in one home took a vow to remain in the Magdalen home for life.[18] She says that it is possible that the nuns suffered the same kind of abuse as the Magdalens, that their lives were very like the nuns' lives. The nuns took vows that governed their lives; the vow of poverty included stipulations on accommodation, common life and work. The vow of chastity included a prohibition on all relationships, sexual and otherwise, both inside and outside the convent.

The vow of obedience covered all aspects of religious life, and encouraged dependency, which led to a lack of maturity. There were many similarities between the two lifestyles and not least in their inability to live independent lives outside the institution. She fails to see that nuns were free to leave while the police brought the Magdalens back if they attempted to escape.

The Magdalens often express their angry feelings and openly act them out. Mary laughs as she speaks about this. How can she laugh? One wonders where the nuns' angry feelings are expressed and if they are projected on to the Magdalens, making them angrier and freeing the nuns from their feelings. It is possible that the Magdalens carried the shadow side of the nuns in order to keep the nuns' repressed feelings of anger and sexuality hidden from conscious knowledge.

The nuns were identified with the Virgin Mary; they had a vow of chastity, the 'angelic virtue' and remained pure. The Magdalens had transgressed, by having illicit sexual contact and were by implication impure, bad and unholy. The split in the Gospels between the Virgin Mary and Mary Magdalen, between good and bad, God and the Devil, saint and sinner was, it seems, played out in bold relief in the lives of those who lived in religious institutions, especially where a Magdalen laundry was attached to the convent.

To retain their perceived position of perfection the nuns needed the Magdalens to offset it, and to act as receptacles for their projections. Any expression of rebellion on the part of the Magdalens had to be quelled, and any transgressions representing the repressed aspects of the nuns had to be punished. There was no place for a third position that would have revealed the underlying, unconscious and repressed aspects of both groups and led to a form of thinking where the whole is acknowledged as containing both the bad and the good.

The same problems of untrained and frustrated staff arise in the residential childcare homes. Before Mary experiences the reality of these homes she thought she would have liked to do this work. When she meets three distressed children she no longer expresses this desire. She relates this heartbreaking meeting without any expression of emotion or comment on the suffering of these children. The encounter may have evoked some painful and unbearable feelings that could not be acknowledged because of her past where she had to live separated from her parents because there were too many children to be cared for. As a result, these feelings had to be kept out of consciousness. Mary often has difficulty in being empathic, but she was in a position to put more educated staff into these children's homes and she did nothing.

She reveals the value system in the convent. Teachers were educated. The teacher was more important than the sister who worked in the industrial school and there was little care for the education of the less privileged nun and child. Mary mentions a practice that was the norm, which her sister, as principal, forbade. Sisters were willing to take children out of school to do jobs. The in-service for sisters who worked in the industrial schools first began in the 1970s.

The division of the nuns into those who were educated and taught in the more public schools, and those who were uneducated and worked in the hidden laundries and industrial schools with the most deprived and despised members of society, was bound to have implications for the care provided in these institutions, and for the self-esteem of the nuns who worked there. At one point the teachers also taught without training but eventually the State demanded it. Why did the State ignore the Magdalen instituitions and the industrial schools? The State turned a blind eye in order to maintain the system of keeping undesirable women and children locked away, out of sight, and in addition it benefitted from cheap laundry services.

Mary is the only nun in the group who has been a Mother General and she had 200 nuns under her jurisdiction. She blocked the possibility of thinking by activity. She represents the dutiful nun who is prepared to carry out every task without feeling or questioning. She will never rock the boat and her compliance to those in higher authority and her lack of creative thinking make her a safe bet to run the institution. She was in a position to make changes when she was in charge, but there is little evidence of that. She is a good woman and she will not inspire undue fear nor will she disturb the universe.

Mary's Story:

A lot of the men went to England

I was born in the south of Ireland and when my father was transferred to the Midlands the family moved and I remained in the south with my grandparents. There was no other young person there. Now I often wondered why I was down there. At home there were three more born after me and the fifth was coming so I suppose my parents thought I'd be minded down there and out of the way. I started school there and I spent my first year in a lay school and I loved it. Then I returned home and continued my primary school. In secondary school there were only two lay teachers. They were past pupils of the school.

When we were going to secondary school the main jobs that were available were the civil service, nursing and teaching, and it was hard enough to get teaching. You either went abroad or stayed at home and married. A lot of the men went to England to get a job to keep the family going. The men were in England while the women were at home, waiting for all this money to come. These men wouldn't have gone to secondary school. It was different for the next generation. You see, we had a Christian Brothers' school in the town as well as the convent so the boys could stay on in school. A lot of them went teaching. They also left the town.

I saw their lovely habits

The convent was there up on the hill and I used to go out for a walk in the evening and I was thinking of the nuns praying and I thought, I am going to give my life to God. Three of my father's sisters were nuns so that probably influenced me and influenced my parents in allowing me to be a religious. At home we got magazines such as the Far East and one from the Sisters of the Sacred Heart. I saw their lovely habits and the work they were doing in China so I was going to China. Then the Maryknoll Sisters came to the school to talk about their work and I remember coming home to my mother who was in bed sick. I showed her this book and I said, 'That's where I'm going out there, never to come back'. I thought that it was going to be great.

In the meantime we had school retreats and when I told the priest leading the retreat about China he said, 'Look, if you go to China you will be doing the same as you would here in Ireland. You think you are going to be baptising babies, black babies, but you'll either be in a school or in a hospital, the same as you would in Ireland.' So he talked me out of it. Thinking back on it, I'm sure the nuns in the convent had been telling him about me. Later one of the teachers in the school gave me a book on the founder of the religious order. Maybe the nuns told her to do it. I was accepted as a postulant although the convent didn't have a policy of taking town girls, or even those around the locality, because they would have had family and friends around. They were encouraged to go to other convents. There was only one other nun from the town in our convent. I entered and thought I would be there for the rest of my life because we had no branch houses.

My second sister was doing an extra year in school, waiting to apply for nursing, and the nuns talked her into becoming a nun and she entered in their convent. As for my third sister, when she was in school the Novice Mistress in the convent told her she would be disobeying the will of God if she didn't enter. I imagine she would have entered but not in that convent. My youngest sister was born in 1941 and she also entered the convent. My two brothers joined the Christian Brothers at fourteen years old. My second brother said he just drifted along and then he saw it wasn't for him at all. He left and married.

She took me by the hand

Two of us entered the same day. They sent me out to teach Catechism to second class as a postulant. On reception day we were in white veils and dresses. I had my mother's wedding dress and her veil. Then we had a spiritual year and I loved that. We had nice readings except, of course, for Rodriquez. But we had a lovely book based on Scripture, written by a nun. I loved that now. I remember her describing the busy day that Jesus had. They were all so busy that they had no time to eat. The story is in Mark's Gospel.

I was professed in 1949. Now our convent, at that time, was just an autonomous house with no branch houses. They were deciding to buy a house at the sea as a holiday house. The day I was professed, the superior took me by the hand, and she never said a word to anyone, novice mistress or anyone, and she put me sitting in a car and we went to the holiday house because she had a picture of Our Lady that she was going to enthrone in this house. It was a holiday house for the first few years. Then they opened it as a secondary school.

It was capitation until the 1970s

I was called to train as a primary teacher the following summer. I was happy enough to go. All I could think of was teaching in the baby room and matchboxes and things you would have to make. The superior at the time said, 'Just get your legs out of it and we'll be happy', so there was no pressure on me at all. I went and I must say I liked it. When I entered there were very few of the nuns trained and all were teaching. It was only when I arrived in sixth class that I had the first teacher who was trained. The nuns weren't paid individually at that time. They received a capitation grant based on the number of pupils so they could have as many teachers as they wanted. Some of them were superannuated. This continued until the 1970s. Normally, you would have eight classes in primary school and we were a five-teacher school so there were five trained teachers and three who were untrained. They were JAMs (junior assistant mistresses). They had experience. Maybe the Department of Education turned a blind eye. After my training I was ready to start.

In walks a cigire

So June came and July came and I had not been allocated a class. The whole summer holidays passed and our superior went to Lourdes. They all went back to school and I still hadn't a class. So she came back and sent for Clare, who taught Junior Infants at the time, and myself. She told Clare she was being transferred and she told me I was going into Clare's class in the baby room on the following Monday. I had no preparation of any kind. So Clare had her syllabus and I went out to school with her syllabus. And in walks a *cigire* (inspector). He was a very strict man. I suppose he knew it was my first day. He was a tall man with glasses and when he opened the door some of the children started to cry and some of them came up and grabbed me. I had no idea what was wrong. I discovered afterwards that some of them had been in school before the summer holidays and a medical doctor had come and had given them an injection. I couldn't explain to the inspector why the children were upset.

That particular day I had another little lad and it was his first day in school, a bubbly little lad, and the inspector stood over him and he looked down at him and he said, 'collect yourself'. And I don't think he has collected himself even to this day. He didn't have any idea of what he was being told. The inspector didn't understand children.

Far away from the bishop

My sisters and I were not in the same diocese until after the convents were amalgamated. One went to England and the other went to the USA but I kept in touch with them through phone and writing. I suppose our letters were read too. At that time the superiors read all letters, those coming in and those going out. In holiday time we all met at home. We entered in convents that were far away from the bishop so we had great freedom. It was the people near him who were under his eye all the time. He came for visitation and we went in and he would ask questions about the books we were using and things like that. He came over to us on a holiday and we behaved ourselves. When we became a diocese the superiors from the main convent started to tell us what the bishop had said. He controlled us to a degree. He would say what time we had to be in at and all that, but there were some rules and you wouldn't know whether he made them or not. It could have been convenient to blame the bishop for rules.

We had our suggestions for chapter

Then in 1969 I was made superior in the house. We had a centenary coming up in 1972 and the house needed a lot of doing up. We were carrying around basins and ewers and the older sisters were going around at night trying to bring water up to their rooms. So we got hot and cold water in the rooms and wardrobes and carpet on the floor and all the little things that you would need for a bit of comfort. Things were beginning to change at that time. At Mass the priest faced the people so we had to get the chapel renovated. Then we had to update our constitutions. It was very dry stuff, the rewriting of these constitutions. Three of us were sent to do our degrees at weekends. I had forgotten that.

Father James appeared on the scene to facilitate the changes and we were off to meetings. We had our first diocesan chapter in June of 1972. We had our suggestions for chapter. The three things we decided on were: three nights at home, the use of bicycles and experiment with the habit. Imagine! Oh Lord! We laughed. As he left Father James said, 'It's over to you now, you've to make the decisions'. Then we had the elections. Before this the superiors of the three houses in the diocese used to meet to prepare for the chapter. We had planned that we would have it in a hotel. The bishop heard the word 'hotel'. No, no hotel! We had it in a conference centre. When he heard we were thinking of amalgamating and electing a Mother General he was suggesting that the three of us should take it in turn! He hadn't a clue.

Why did I let myself be elected?

At this chapter I was elected Mother General. The blood nearly runs out of my body when I think of it. That day, I will never forget it. I came from the smallest convent in the diocese. I remember going into the chapel and I was asked to carry a missal or something and they were singing 'Abide with Me' and 'hold thou thy cross before my closing eyes' and the tears were running right down my face. I'll never forget that day, thinking of leaving my small convent. I found that very hard and what I found hardest was that Father James was saying that once you leave a place you cut yourself off totally. There was no place for feelings. That nearly killed me altogether because I was leaving my friends. I didn't keep in touch with them. I look back on it and I say always keep in touch with your friends and never cut them off. But I'm very friendly with them now. I'm free to do it.

Why did I let myself be elected? At the chapter we had our minds made up who we were going to vote for and the next thing the nun who was nominated stood up and said she wasn't accepting the nomination. We thought it was terrible. We had to turn around and start again. After that I said to myself, well, if enough people have gone to the trouble of thinking that they want me I won't say no because I couldn't stand up and say, 'no thank you'.

We soon found a new place

The five were elected that day, the Mother General and the team. We met that evening and it was a nice kind of happy occasion. We had to find a generalate, a place to live and work. We were told that down at the Magdalen there was a lot of space, a separate entrance and so on, and of course, without seeing it, we voted. Well it taught me a lesson: never vote for something that you don't know about or see. So we came in to find two big empty rooms and a toilet and a wash hand basin and that was all that was in it. Then they gave us bedrooms upstairs. It was very difficult. We had no privacy. Then we had to get a porch and an entrance. And some of the people in the house did not understand at all. Some of the sisters would come to visit and they'd be told only superiors were allowed to visit. Ah, 'twas hilarious! You see, two of us could be in a room and it seemed to be private but we didn't realise we could be heard outside or next door or whatever. So, that was that. We soon found a new place.

There was nothing of good that brought that pair today

Then Father James said that I was to go to the States almost immediately because there were two communities that I had to get to know because they had to have new superiors by the first week in June. I had to get to know everyone and who was suitable. So I went to the States to two houses where I knew nobody. Representatives of the two houses met me. And, of course, they were bent on bringing me places. In both houses the fear was that they would be brought home. That didn't enter my head and they had a groundsman in one of the houses and he would be chatting me during the day, telling me the great work the sisters were doing, and everything. That was 1973, and I had to keep in mind who was willing to take on leadership in the two houses, and I think there could have been a change of principals too.

Then I came back to get ready for all of these changes at home at the beginning of June. I had to visit every house. My first councillor and I went to a particular house for a social visit, and there was an old sister there and when we left she said, 'There was nothing of good that brought that pair today'. And you wouldn't believe it, within a week we were thinking of changing someone there. Father James made it difficult because all the announcements had to be done on the same day. I had to go from one house to another. That was a difficult time because the team didn't know the sisters. We had two on the council who did, but they might never have lived with them. The minute I arrived in office I had all these property developers coming to see me. They had come to my predecessors and they told them they were going to have a new administration. And oh, to tell them that we weren't going to sell and that we needed it for ourselves!

I found it all very difficult. I found myself in an awfully lonely space at that time. I felt like Christ in the garden and they were all gone. I had nobody. I remember I had to tell a sister that the hostel she had run for years was going to be closed and sold. I had a first councillor, at that time, but I don't know where she was. It was something I had to do on my own. And I found that difficult. During that time the whole thing was so confidential I couldn't share things with others, and even though some would have been willing to carry the burden with me I couldn't share it.

I'll be growing the daisies

In January 1976 I was going to the States again, that was for the next set of visitation and my mother had fallen and she was in hospital and I had gone to visit her New Year's Day and I remember she said,

'You'll be coming home?'

'I'll be coming home on the twenty-third of February.'

'I'll be growing the daisies.'

'They don't come up as fast as that.'

So I went to the States and I was visiting some relatives and the ground was thick with snow so I was grounded in Boston for a few days. Then I got word that my mother had died and I was on the next plane home. I was crying on the plane and this man beside asked, 'Are you going back after the holidays', so I told him. He was extremely nice and gave me the use of the phone. He was a priest and he said he would say Mass for my mother. She died on Friday and this was Saturday evening. She was buried on the Monday. I was sorry for my father.

My father was living alone and my sister, who had entered after me, used to go down home and sleep there at night. She was gone in the morning before he'd get up and she corrected her copies when she went down at night. I went to the States again and when I came home my father had had a stroke. I came in from the airport and he said, 'I'm sorry to disappoint you that I wasn't there to meet you.' I said, 'You needn't worry Dad, I'll always have someone to meet me.'

My two brothers were up with him the night before and he was having a cup of tea and he said, 'Nobody can look after me like yourselves,' and the nurse, who was a friend of ours, was in next door and she said, 'You won't be able to mind him. I'll get him into hospital.' The ambulance came within a half an hour. Dad went into hospital then and he died later that year. So those are my two American visits. We had another chapter and I was re-elected for another three years.

The laundry was still open

As I already said after the first chapter, in 1973, the team was living in the Magdalen convent. By this time I think the era of abuse had passed but the laundry was still open and the women were still there. Although it is now closed there are women still in it. Some of them had strange stories.

Women were sent into the Magdalen by the parish priest or by parents if the girl became pregnant. Sometimes there was a fear that parents would interfere with a girl. There is one woman there whose father had died and she lived in the house with an uncle. She was fourteen and I think she was raped. She had a child and she was taken in. Some of the women had no children. Children were never born in the Magdalen down here. They were born in some of the other homes. After the birth they came back without their babies. The babies were never brought here. It is said that the women weren't let to see their babies or children who were here in care, and the children weren't allowed to see their mothers. I don't believe it but maybe it could have happened.

The only story, in living memory, of a baby being born in the Magdalen here was in the sixties. A pregnant girl came in and the nuns didn't know it. The nun in charge would go up in the morning and call them. They were in dormitories and there were wash hand basins all along so that they all washed beside one another. They came down to the chapel for morning prayers. They knew the prayers by heart. Then they had Mass, thanksgiving and then breakfast. Then they went down to work in the laundry. The women had this big chapel down in the Magdalen and part of it was the sisters' place and this area down here was for the girls. They were a kind of secular order or something. They were semi-sisters and they were down here and this is my own experience of it. The women were not paid for their work and the nuns were also working down there in the laundry. Then there were lay people who came in and there were a few men looking after the boilers. Some of these nuns who worked in the laundry were not educated. I'd say the kind of abuse the Magdalens complain about was something that maybe the rest of us were suffering from too. The life they were living was very like our lives. Like them, we were often in dormitories in the noviceship with just screens between us.

On this particular morning they were all down at Mass and they missed a girl and when they went up she had given birth to a baby and that was the only time I heard of a baby being there. The nun in charge nearly fainted because she had done a lot to upgrade the place. She had done away with uniforms by the time I came. She was a bossy kind of person but she had a good heart. She wouldn't abuse them but she would boss them around and they wouldn't like her even though she was very caring of them. She used to buy things for them. I know some of the sisters who lived with her and they were afraid of her.

I saw the film *The Magdalene Sisters*. It was dreadful. It wasn't true. The film was made because some of the Magdalens complained. Some of these left in the earlier days and they said that they were beaten and possibly interfered with by the priest and the doctor and the gardener. It seemed awful in the film. There were letters being sent in and out.

I think a lot of the Magdalens weren't able to read or write and I don't know if attempts were made to teach them. They should have been taught to read and write but an awful lot of them were slow. They weren't really fully mature at all. They weren't able to think for themselves, but whether they were like that coming in or not, I don't know.

Because I wasn't there

It seems that the women, poor creatures, would be very angry and vexed and they would be fighting among themselves. One of the nuns was saying that one could throw an iron at another but whatever happened it was generally among themselves. They were talking about their hair being cut if they did something wrong. Now that could be true, that a sister would have cut their hair. I'm not too sure because I wasn't there.

Now at one stage the women were given permission to leave, to go home. Some did but others came back. There were a few who were back when I was there. They couldn't live outside because of the life they were leading up to that time. Two of them went out to work for the sisters in the local convent and they were paid. Now they are both not well and they are in a nursing home, being paid for by the sisters, by the province. One of them had a child, a boy, and she keeps in touch and he used to come and visit her and take her to England. She kept up with him.

There are only very few of them there at the moment. They have a lovely place, a beautiful place, new rooms to themselves and a lovely day room and a nice dining room and a special cook for themselves and they have a tiny little laundry. When they got the new place, I was with Sister Teresa, and one of the women was showing us around and she said, 'Wait till you see what they call a laundry now'. It was such a little place in comparison to the other. But they have a very nice place there now and they have their own Mass down below and the sisters go down to their place.

Most of the nuns were not trained for the work

I had come from a small convent knowing nothing about childcare. A new manager had gone up there to the childcare home.

She was a nurse and from her time on things changed. Before that that there were sisters there who would have beaten these children. There were two sisters there and I barely knew them before they died and the nuns said that they beat the children. I find it very hard to reconcile that with religious life. I ask myself why? I don't know, but maybe it was frustration that they had all these children around them and they weren't able to mind them, and the same with those Magdalen girls if they weren't treated well. Most of the nuns were not trained for this work.

I remember the first day I went into the home and I opened a door into this room. There were three little children there and they were screaming, they were running out and screaming 'Daddy, Daddy, Daddy', and they gripped me! I discovered afterwards that their father hadn't visited them for six months and then he had come and left again. I discovered that some of the children there were a result of incest. One family had the same mother but different fathers because the husband was getting men to pay for his wife's services. That was a whole new experience for me.

The nuns were untrained because there was no childcare training. Later they were getting in-service training. On the other hand, teachers were trained. I could see that these uneducated nuns were often frustrated. There was a big number of children up there crying and someone needed to go up and look after them and people like me had other things to do. I could see that all right.

The children didn't go out to the primary school. They had a school on site. My sister was the principal and she was very caring of them because the nuns would want to take them out of school to do jobs and she just wouldn't have it. My sister was one of those who had to appear before the tribunal. A young woman accused her of calling her too early and pulling her hair. At the tribunal she didn't say that at all. The solicitor said, 'Sister is here now', and she turned and said, 'How are you Sister?' But even if she did pull her hair, which she didn't, it was only an ordinary thing. Another young woman said that somebody had hit her with a grill and she was scarred for life. Now in the course of an examination she admitted that she had fallen off a chair and hurt her leg. Some of these cases are unbelievable but I would say that there was harshness all right.

I'm thinking of the provincial leaders now. Maybe they never worked or put a foot inside a childcare home and they have to take all this responsibility for what was done by our order. I think that's very hard on them. You know, if you do something yourself it's nearly easier to own up to it and acknowledge it. But to have to take responsibility in public for what others have done is very difficult, even though there is none of it happening now or hasn't been happening for years.

We had a great four years

When I finished as Mother General I had freedom. I'll never forget when I was on holidays looking out at the sea and hills and everything and I felt, oh, that I hadn't a trouble in the world. Then I took a sabbatical and I joined a small group in a house. We prepared for it together and we worked there together. It was great. We had four great years. We could share everything. We had our differences and everything but still it was a very up-building time. You could depend on the group. But that was a good time. You know I felt their support and companionship. I found the life itself and the people around me very spiritual. I found my time in the generalate very spiritual too. We were meeting with others from other dioceses and I'd say we were getting good spiritual input, and I wanted that for the sisters as well.

During that time I was back on the general council and we set up boards of management in every school. It wasn't too easy because we had a lot of opposition. We eventually got that done. I was chairperson in a lot of them and being chair has more to do than chairing the meetings. You have to be responsible for interviewing and for appointments and for all of these things. So I found that extremely difficult. We had a vacancy in one school and I set up everything and going into it the superior said to me, 'You have to appoint Ms. X'. The applicants were all lay people now. I had two independent people interviewing with me and the two were for somebody else, and we couldn't accept their choice so we had to say that it was incomplete or inconclusive. That was very problematic.

Then I was sent to a community of about eighteen nuns and I didn't like the idea of going at all. It was my first time now in a big community in about twenty years. Wherever I was I would have been responsible with everybody else for shopping and cooking and doing all these things. I was very upset leaving the small house but at the same time there was work to be done and out I went. My sister was there and I remember talking to her and she was telling me what a nice community it was. I know she would have preferred if I hadn't come out. There were a good few older sisters there and I got some jobs to do going out. First of all to do up the house, to make it fire safe, was number one, and number two to have it suitable for elderly sisters. There were steps all over the place so I suggested ramps. This sister said, 'I hate ramps, do you?' I said, 'Hate them or not we can't be climbing steps.' We had a meeting about a lift. Yes, we needed a lift. Next meeting, no, we didn't need any lift. There were always older people in this house. So finally anyway we got the lift and from the day the lift was put in the sister who was totally against it never put her foot on the stairs again.

No place under the sun

After that assignment I joined a small house again and I was organising things there until one day I met one of the council and she was saying that it would be better for me to leave that place because there was too much work to be done. That was a shock to me now because I was being asked to leave a place rather than go and do something. I did a directed retreat and then I looked around because I had nowhere to go. This was the only house that I could think of. So I met the superior in the house and I asked if there was a room here. I did this when I shouldn't because you see change has to be negotiated now by the authorities. The house has to be consulted about the new person and so on. I spent a long time weighing the pros and the cons, and when I came it took me a long time to settle and I am beginning to see it has been good for me to come. So I find I have time to myself and I have space that I can call my own and I won't be called down to do this or that. I have every facility in the line of spirituality as well. The Dominicans are around and I love to go to their Mass at half ten. Then they come in to us once a month for anointing and the new man really makes a sacrament out of it. It's lovely. He sings and he goes around and he blesses us. That's the funny thing, I'd have to call here home now. I suppose it is here. There's no place else under the sun.

6

Margaret

'I don't know whether I had a vocation'

Introduction

Margaret is seventy-six years of age. Her mother died after the birth of her younger brother when she was eighteen months old. She and her brother spent most of their young lives being moved around their extended family until their father remarried and they returned home. Margaret has many happy memories of this extended, thrifty, farming family. Her description of her childhood is dominated by food, a sign, perhaps, of her deep loss of a mother's care and love, which she had known for eighteen months.

Margaret's main ambition in life is to be on the move, to travel. Travelling to new places, having new experiences, fills a gap, and bypasses the need for serious reflection. She later extends this to looking after the homeless. She was effectively homeless when her mother died, although she was well looked after. There were many relatives, both male and female, in religious life and it was no surprise when Margaret showed an interest in becoming a nun. However her choice of Australia where one of her cousins was a nun was not acceptable to her father. She had to stay in Ireland. She had invitations from relatives to enter in their convents but a persistent invitation from one novice from the local area won the day.

In order to travel Margaret was prepared to join an order that ran a Magdalen laundry. She talks a lot about her home life rather than religious life. This may be an unconscious diversionary tactic, to avoid talking about the essence of religious life and the taboo subject of the Magdalens who were often mothers separated from their babies. Margaret has learned to protect herself from unwanted feelings. Splitting off unwanted inner parts simplifies and impoverishes the self, and allows the individual to 'travel light',[19] but with a lessening of the capacity to be responsible for feelings and actions.

Margaret knew nothing about the order she joined except that they had a Magdalen laundry. She speaks about this institution from the perspective of a young girl of the time. Even now she feels she should not be revealing how chilling it was to pass by or to leave in some laundry. Stories were circulated but they cannot be recounted. Chinese whispers? She is physically affected by her memories but she has split off her knowledge. Then she is not worried by what she knows, but she is lost for words and cannot finish what she begins to say. She reacts at the thought of seeing the women when she handed in the odd tablecloth to be laundered for Christmas. The women washed society's dirty linen so that they could celebrate the birth of Christ with impunity. At an unconscious level they cleansed away the dirt, while at the same time holding something frightening for society, something that could not be put into words. These things cannot be spoken about. Margaret turns a blind eye to what she knows about the way the Magdalens were ill-treated, although she admits to having read a book lately that revealed their 'tough' lives. The book is an admission that she knows things but it gives her some distance from the subject.

Turning a blind eye raises the question of corporate responsibility for wrongdoing; is everyone to blame for not seeing or can those who did no wrong be exonerated? It also raises the question of whether one can be guilty through inaction. Margaret says that the nuns are all under the one umbrella since the convents amalgamated, but she takes no responsibility for what is written in the media. She, like many others, conflates the Magdalen laundries and the industrial schools. While speaking of the Magdalens she says that she never stood in an orphanage in her life. This points to the close connection, in the mind, between the mothers who were in the Magdalen and their children who were in the industrial schools. It raises many questions and often, as in Margaret's case, it leads to confusion. The stories about the laundry were in the public domain so the society of the time cannot be entirely exonerated for what was happening there. Of course, Margaret is not personally responsible for the Magdalen laundries and the industrial schools, so it could be said that her denial mirrors that of society. It is also the way many of the nuns who were not working in these institutions deal with the abuse. The question of corporate responsibility is a thorny issue.

Now, in her old age, Margaret lives in this convent because it is conveniently near her family of origin. In the past she chose the order because it offered the possibility of travel. Some of the Magdalens live in the refurbished basement of this convent and there is a hint of dehumanisation in the way Margaret describes them. They are 'lovely creatures' if you are careful and do not antagonise them. If you antagonise them they would attack viciously. They provide a receptacle for Margaret's projection of her unacceptable 'creature' parts, her primitive envy and her anger.

One of Margaret's deciding factors in choosing this order, in spite of its close connections with the Magdalens, was the possibility of travel. The nuns had convents outside Ireland while the order where Margaret attended secondary school did not have any convents abroad. In addition, a group of young women from the area were entering there. She rather casually states that she went there 'in the heel of the hunt' but she 'doesn't know why'. A supernatural calling is certainly in doubt, and on reflection Margaret wonders if she had a vocation at all and adds that she probably got it along the way.

Margaret was sent to teach as a postulant and learned that to be cross was all that was required to be a good teacher. In this she colluded with the convent culture that control had to be maintained at all times. Her experience of the cross nun at school was that it 'frightened the life' out of her so she is not without some inner conflict about doing as she is told. She quickly splits off her own better judgement and tries to compensate by being cross but fair.

Without any choice in the matter she was sent to university and she spent many years teaching in various secondary schools. The convent, at this time, had a rather perverse way of looking at talent. It was thought that developing individual talents would lead to hubris and the sin of pride, so one was not asked to do what one liked or was good at. Depriving one of choice in one's career or lifework sets up a struggle within the individual between a true, inner sense of value, what one might like to be, where one's talents lies and a value that is not true to the self.[20] After Vatican II Margaret was able to be true to herself, by choosing the work she wanted with the homeless in England.

Her work with the homeless began when she was on a career break and continued later in spite of the dismissive attitude of the superior. She was no longer prepared to accept authority unchallenged as she had done with her father. When she accompanies an alcohol-addicted Irishman home to his mother for Christmas she does not consider the personal wishes of either. By enacting this scenario one wonders *if she is trying to satisfy, by proxy, some deep longing within her to be united with the mother she lost at eighteen months, and for whom she allegedly searched in cupboards.*

In 1997 she satisfied her inner compulsion to travel to Australia courtesy of her family who also gave her five hundred pounds pocket money. Since then Margaret has used her allowance to visit many countries, including going on a holiday cum retreat to Mallorca. Apart from the mention of the retreat, there is only one other allusion to spirituality.

When she enters the convent Margaret has her agenda and she is prepared to tolerate the demands and inconveniences of convent life to get what she wants. She is diligent in executing the work of the order but embraces the convent culture of controlling her pupils by crossness, by inspiring fear, which she modifies by being fair. She denies her concerns and unwanted feelings by projecting them on to others, leaving her free to pursue her agenda. Margaret got what she wanted from becoming a nun, and perhaps not surprisingly, she would not call the convent 'home'. Home for her is with her brother and his wife.

Margaret's Story:

Home life was very basic

My mother died in 1933, a fortnight after my brother, John, was born. I was eighteen months old at the time. I don't remember a bit of it in the wide world. My Dad said I opened every cupboard, every press, and every place you could open searching for her, pulling out tins and saucepans and pots and pans, but I don't remember a bit of it, needless to say. It must have been heartbreaking for him.

John stayed with an auntie and I stayed with my grandmother and I think I became a little selfish. I was the only one, and I was spoiled. I had everything of my own. Later John and I were together with an auntie. She was like another mother. I used to call her 'mammy' and Jim was her husband and I called him 'daddy' even though I had my own Dad down at home but there was great friendship there. We were very happy and our Dad visited us regularly. He was a farmer and farming at that time was hard, all manual work. I have memories of my grandmother who was lovely to me. Once she brought me to the races. She had a lovely big brown shawl with tassels on it and they're all fashionable again.

That time at home life was very basic but a very, very healthy life. We lived in a lovely thatched house. There were pink flowers in the back garden, and an orchard, plenty of apples and blackcurrants. My aunt had this huge pan and she would make jam. We had a lovely turlough. This is vividly in my mind. The place was full of rocks. We loved playing around these rocks. 'This rock is my rock and this is yours,' this carry on. There were no bicycles or cars. We had a sidecar.

At Christmas we never had turkey. The turkeys were sold, a gentleman would come in before Christmas and he'd set up the weighing scales in the kitchen and the turkeys would be weighed and they would be bought and they were very pricey. At the time it was keeping the household and the family going. This would be pre-war now of course. We never had a turkey to eat; I never ate turkey until I entered.

We had Santa in wartime as well

The war came and rationing was a big thing. Everything was rationed but my auntie was a great housekeeper, very economical. Tea was thirty shillings a pound and was kept in a press in the kitchen. It was impossible to get but she would get it, where I don't know. It would be spared, rationed, not that we were great tea drinkers. We had geese and we loved to eat them. They would be absolutely delicious. We'd all be there getting ready. Auntie would make black pudding and it was lovely. We had the giblets a few days before Christmas. We had lovely potato stuffing. The goose was put into an oven on an open fire, on a big iron crane. Little coals called *griosach* were put over the lid and under the oven. The goose would come out of that absolutely delicious. And there was no talk of poisoning or anything at that time I can tell you. Auntie also made a plum pudding. That time they had big, big raisins, huge! For me, whether it's nostalgic or not, the taste was different. And they never heated the plum pudding. It was cut into slices and left over in the parlour in a big dish. When visitors came they'd get a glass of wine or whisky or whatever with the slice of plum pudding, decent slices.

We had Santa in the wartime as well. I had an uncle, a priest, and he would come and say, 'Girls, what do you want for Christmas?' I usually wanted a doll. I got a blue bicycle. It was brand new and I was delighted cycling to school about five miles away. I remember coming down the hill between cows' hind legs. I'll never forget how many times I fell off that bicycle but we all learnt to cycle anyhow, which was great after falling so many times. I got a *Curly Wee* book long ago and little jumpers and little aprons and little dresses and so on. They were very good to me. I could do nothing wrong.

Uncle (the priest) had malaria after coming from the missions and couldn't go out to Mass. He'd say, 'Breads now, Margaret, because I want a Mass in the house.' I didn't know the difference between bread and consecrated hosts. I really didn't. I was first or second year in secondary school. I remember going into the shop in town and getting Camel cigarettes for him. We had coupons for everything and no tyres for your bicycle, no petrol or anything!

Nothing at all wasted

Another thing at that time was the killing the pig. You see, meat was not bought at all. The bacon came from your own pig. Oh, yeah, when you killed the pig the custom was to go around with a basket or bag and you'd give the fillet to all the neighbours. It was the inside of the pig, they'd cut it out, and it was absolutely delicious. I never ate pork like it anyway. An odd time I'd have pork over there at the hotel but you'd never get anything like it. When the relations came around you always had some. We'd give fruitcake and eggs to all the houses for the stations (Mass in the house).

My auntie had a hand machine, a sewing machine and the material was in a big roll and she'd make dresses. You'd buy flour in big white bags, 'Heart's Delight' would be written on the bag. You can still get that flour now. Auntie would get boiling water and boil the bags and get the stains, marks, off them. She'd make little slips and knicks for us. They would be dyed a kind of mauve. They were lovely. So we had our own little ways, things were done so economically then. Nothing, nothing wasted. Nothing at all wasted.

In post-war times you didn't have that much at home either. We were never hungry. Out on a farm we had plenty to eat. Somebody asked yesterday, 'What's *caiscín?' Caiscín* (wholewheat) was when my uncle brought wheat to the local mill, and brought it back ground, crushed, and my auntie would put a white sheet on the stone floor in the kitchen. We'd have to empty the bags of ground wheat and spread it out. It was hot. You would cool it so it wouldn›t get lumpy. You gathered it off on the floor then and it would be put into bags and kept for as long as you needed it.

It made wonderful brown bread. We had good food you see. I hardly ever remember being sick.

The May Queen

I started school in a little country school, and I was very happy coming back to my lunch every day across a field. In summertime we'd go in our bare feet from May on. Have you ever heard of the May Queen? We'd get one lassie to do it. She always had lovely knitted dresses, which she wore to school when we were in first or second class. There'd be a lot of primroses. We picked the primroses and put them into the dress and decorated the whole dress sleeves, bodice, collar everything and she went into the master next door and she got sixpence and that was a lot of money that time. I remember the master telling us about the children of Lir. The headmaster said, 'Anyone who comes into me called Aodh, Conn, Fiachra or Fionnuala I'll give them sixpence'. But no child ever came in. They might today. At that time you were called after your grandmother or your uncles and aunts.

We weren't too happy with our stepmother

I did the usual subjects at primary school. I remember going around the schoolyard saying 'suffered under Pontius Pilate died and was buried'. I didn't know what I was talking about. I was a very young child, about say five or six. I remember my father at night and the pink catechism, twopenny catechism, a penny or tuppence I think. It had a pink cover and in the back was 'I'll sing a hymn to Mary, Mother of my God' and he teaching me that and 'tower of ivory' and I didn't know what I was saying no more than the pussycat. I forgot to say my father got married again, a second time, in 1941 and we went back home again. Kind of hard going back again and we weren't too happy with our stepmother for a while.

Six of us, six girls, started secondary school in 1945 and did the Leaving Cert in 1950. My own experience is that some nuns were cross. Some would frighten the life out of you. One nun would take the cincture (leather belt) and bang it down on the desk. 'Stop talking,' she would roar at you. They weren't that cross when you think of the times. You accepted these things.

I don't know whether I had a vocation

I wanted to enter in Australia. Why Australia? I don't know. I had cousins out there and I was longing to go to Perth, Australia because one of the sisters, Sister Brigid, was a first cousin of my father. She was reared in our house. My Grandmother reared her because her mother died when she was young and I used to write to her and I said I'd love to go to Australia. I spent the year after the Leaving Cert writing behind their backs at home. I said to my father, 'I am going to Australia'.

'Why Australia? If you want to be a nun you'll have to enter in Ireland.'

That's a time that you did what you were told and I did what I was told and entered in a convent less than thirty miles from home because there was a crowd there from my home place. Seven entered, people from home, people I knew well. It was strange I don't know whether I had a vocation. I probably got it along the way. At home, as a youngster, I was brought up on religion because a lot of nuns were coming home, coming and going, and a lot of relations were priests on the missions as well.

Mary Rose was instrumental in getting me to go to her convent. She was a novice there and she came from our village. I had letter after letter from her saying, 'Please come and join us'. I hadn't a notion of joining those sisters, not a notion in the wide world. In the heel of the hunt I entered there. Why? I don't know why. I didn't like the sisters at all. I didn't know them. They had a laundry and even as a youngster coming in and out from home, up the road a few miles, I didn't, I shouldn't be saying this out loud, passing here I used to shudder, shivers would go up your back, you associated it with the Magdalens. You'd hear stories and you would come in with the odd tablecloth for Christmas. You know, you know, that kind of thing gets, eh! You would see the women. You got this feeling that this was, eh! I hadn't a clue from Adam except that the women worked very hard down there. We had nothing like that where I went to school.

I was the only one who had a watch

I had to leave everything after me when I entered, including my mother's watch. I couldn't use her gold watch. I had to have a silver one. So that broke my heart. I wore it in school. I was the only one who had a watch. My friend would write on a piece of paper 'time?' and I would write the time and hand it back to her. It broke my heart to leave that lovely gold watch. I gave it to a niece. It was a lovely gold watch, real gold. 'Margaret, you can't have it,' said the Novice Mistress. That was it. You can have anything now. It's so different, silly I suppose, rules and rules.

We were six months as postulants. We wore little white bonnets, lacy bonnets with a little black veil hanging from it and a long black dress. It was imperative that you always had your umbrella, sun, winter, summer, whatever, because the lace on the bonnet would collapse if it got wet. We thought we were the bee's knees.

As postulants, at eighteen years of age, we were sent out to teach. The Novice Mistress said, 'You with the frilly bonnet, Margaret, now you take the Inter Certs, teach them Geography, you know, get them honours'. She knew I got honours in Geography. I had no teaching qualification. And she said, 'You are the real thing, be cross', and I was as cross as could be. That was the definition of a good teacher, to be as cross as could be. I kept that up for a long time, you know. *Smacht* (control), that was it. I would query the teaching part of it but I liked it. I enjoyed it. I was very strict. I'm sure my past pupils would say, 'You were fair'. I love to hear that. 'You were fair.' I wouldn't make fish of one and flesh of another for all Ireland. I have heard that, in some places, if you were the doctor's daughter you were away with it. I didn't approve of that at all. Doctor's daughter or not, you got it from me just as much as any other one's daughter. I was strict but you had to be, in a secondary school. I wouldn't survive twenty-four hours in a secondary school today.

Twenty-three of us in the novitiate

In the novitiate we had great fun, no television, no radio no newspapers. After reception it was spiritual year – strict, no visitors, not many anyway, letters just once a month. First Sunday was always a retreat Sunday at the time. And then I'm scattered again. We had a big Novice Mistress; she was a huge woman, heart of gold. With this exterior you'd expect a really severe person but she wasn't. We'd get lots of presents and she would say, 'The thing is now put them into the press', and she would give them out to us in the evening. Everything was prefaced by, 'The thing is now'.

After spiritual year, I was sent to primary school teaching. First class for two years, one as a white veil and one as a professed sister, and I loved it. Then the Novice Mistress said, 'Margaret, you're going to the university to do your degree', so that was it. The year 1959 was my degree year. Then for the Higher Diploma, I had to stay at home. A taxi took us up and down to the university. We taught all day and went up for the evening lectures. So we did our teaching practice at home and a lot more because we taught on Saturday as well. And on Sunday morning we did our study, supervised study.

We had about forty nuns altogether at the time, community nuns, and twenty-three of us in the novitiate. You didn't dare look at a community nun, strict Canon Law. You didn't dream of looking at them. They would talk to you. They weren't supposed to but you couldn't hold a conversation. It didn't affect me much. It was hard on the five who had been taught by these sisters. To me it makes no sense meeting people on the stairs and your head down, your eyes cast down, as we were told.

You're like the Wren boys

We hadn't a penny in the novitiate. I remember getting two half crowns going to Dublin with the children and I thought it was excellent, two half-crowns, two half-crowns and we were happy. I can't remember being down. We laughed over it. We thought it was great. We used to come home for one day at Christmas, this was after first profession, and we'd come back with a load of money. The people had the height of respect for you; you were a special person. Everyone would be putting money into your hands, now it was the green pound at that time. Going from house to house, and uncles, aunts, cousins everyone giving money. I remember the Novice Mistress saying, 'Do you know you're like the Wren boys'.[21] We gave up every penny of it. We'd never see a penny of it, not a penny, even for years later.

All the sixties, seventies to 1985

After Higher Diploma I did one year at home teaching, then I was sent to another convent for ten years, all the sixties. I was very happy and loved it but at first, heartbroken for home, out in a country place a big farm around it. I loved it because it was farming. It was lovely fresh air. We got out, as we did as children, we got out with our big long habits and all the rest of it, got the rake, and turned the hay and picked the potatoes. We had great fun, a crowd of us. I loved every bit of it, to awake in the morning to the sound of the *cailleach*! I had a bicycle there and I could cycle all over the place.

After that I was transferred again for all the seventies to 1985. I loved it and it was nicer again because it was all *tri Gaeilge* (through Irish). I enjoyed it when I got used to it. I loved it altogether beside the lake where we used to go on holiday as novices. Mass, games you name it and I enjoyed it, another country place, lovely area, the tourists don't know about it. Lovely woods there, lovely waterfall, nature trails and it was great. On holidays, as novices, we were there climbing mountains. It was really great, hills not mountains.

It was a fairly small school, about two hundred boarders. I was principal for a while there. Then I said to the Mother General, 'Please get somebody else, I love teaching, I prefer teaching', and the next thing she said, 'Would you like to go to Dunbeg?' I didn't feel a bit like it but I went. That was a bit of shock. My heart was broken because it was a mixed school and it was English-speaking. I wasn't happy there but I settled in. I took French for a bit. I worked a lot in France. I worked in laundries and anywhere I could get work, to pay my way, and I'd come back with cheese, the laughing cow and I'd see it here in the shops!

I got very smart

Then I took a career break and went to Mill Hill in London and loved it. I did all the classes and lectures that were to be done, and enjoyed Old Testament and New Testament and all that. It was lovely, wonderful lecturers there in Mill Hill, thirteen miles outside London. I knew all the undergrounds and how to get them and how to get to the different stations. I got very smart. That was twelve years ago. It was such a different setup. Went to every kind of show, *The Nutcracker* and *Dancing at Lughnasa* and all that I could go to. I enjoyed it. I didn't concentrate too much now on taking out any more degrees. I didn't want them. So a Christian Brother from South Africa and myself went every Tuesday out to that poor area, Quex Road. It was an old Presbyterian Church I think, Methodist, one of these anyway, birds were flying, crows were flying through it and we'd serve dinners, lunches for the homeless every day, mostly Irish, I'm sorry to say. And there'd be tables of them, here as far as the gate, hundreds. Over a hundred anyway, mostly men, and the lady in charge said, 'Don't worry about feeding them, try and get talking to them'. I said I'd love to do this when I finished teaching and retired. In the college you had every nationality. At times we'd go to synagogues and all that kind of thing. We'd get a flavour of everything, which was great.

I'd like to do what you are doing

I returned to Ireland to teach. It was a lovely place but the attitude of the pupils was, 'Sister, fhat (what) good is French?' Two years there and I went back then to that work I did in London. I was sixty-one at that time and I was talking to one of our sisters who was working with the homeless and I said to her, 'Will you tell me about your work in Dublin because when I finish I want to do what you're at. I'd like to do what you're doing.'

'But you're a teacher.'

'No thanks, I want to get away from that now.'

'Don't wait until you're retired, go now, you're too old when you retire. Go now.'

'Maybe I will. I'm thinking about it you know.'

And I did. And I spoke to the superior. She asked, 'Where will you go?'

'I think I'll go to England.'

'England. You? England?'

'Yes.'

'Why?'

'Because.'

'Are you not coming home for Christmas?'

'No I'm not. I'm staying there. I'll just see what Christmas is like on the other side.'

I went to England to stay with our community there. So I was there from 1993 until 2001 and I loved it because it was Irish people all the time. People went over there, men and women, mostly men, working on the roads and canals. I enjoyed it. They spoke the same accents as they did here in Ireland. 'Fhat would I do without you?' I worked first in a hostel, getting lunches, preparing vegetables, and talking to them, of course.

They pawned the suit

Christmas was coming. So this fellow, his name was Seánín, a bottle of methylated spirits in one hand and some kind of beer in the other, mixing, and that was the beverage. The man was nearly poisoned, drinking, drinking all the time. I said, 'Listen, you must write to your mother for Christmas.'

'I'm not able to write.'

'Listen, you're going to write to her. I'm taking you in a card tomorrow, and you'll write on it to your mother'.

So I took him one with a flock of sheep, it might appeal to him. The hand was shaking.

'I'm not able to write. I'm not able to write.'

'You tell me what to write now and I'll write it.'

So I sent the card home and the poor mother, she hadn't got a letter or a card since God knows when. I decided to bring him home to her. So down I went and booked the two places and I got Seánín, who was stocious drunk because his friends heard he was leaving to see his mother, and all the other winos gathered round him and they pawned the suit he had ready to go home. He hadn't a thing and he was footless going home. I brought him anyway. He hadn't a notion where he was because he was so drunk. So I brought him back to his mother and I really enjoyed that. That was seven years ago. I go back there.

There's a bit of life in me yet. I had great friendships there. Always a bed here for me, 'your room is here'. I'll take up on that again. I have been very, very lucky.

I love to travel

The desire to travel is something in my genes and something in the family, even my nieces and nephews have gone all over the place, Thailand, New Zealand, and I am the same. This aunt of mine took me places; we did the shrines of France back in the seventies. She joined Young at Heart and she went on trips to Denmark and other places. She would say, 'Margaret will you not come with me?' I had this longing and I still have. There is something in me that I love travelling, you know, going places. I went to Norway three years ago. I'd love to go to Finland, not Spain, not heat, or sunshine. I was at home the other day and the same thing. They are all travelling here, there and everywhere.

When I was in England I went all over the place, the Holy Land, Austria, Tenerife, not Tenerife it was Mallorca because there were sisters there. And they said, 'Come on, we are going to have a retreat cum holiday'. I said to the parish priest, 'I am going on a retreat to Mallorca'. He nearly tore his hair out laughing. That's where he went with his father, he said, when his mother died. In wintertime, it was ideal. We had a retreat. The sisters brought little leaflets, Evening Prayer and Morning Prayer. We had a priest with us and we had Mass in every hotel we went to. I thought this was great.

Just seven years ago I went to Australia. I had to go because I had some kind of longing, craving. For six weeks. I loved it and my family they gave me money to go. I got five hundred pounts at that time, 1997.

It gives the shivers up my back

We nuns amalgamated our convents in the seventies and now we're all under one umbrella. What it says about us in the papers doesn't affect me in the least. I had nothing to do with the Magdalens until I landed here five years ago. I knew about them when I was growing up. Those that were here all their lives they love it. They love it. Selfish of me to say but it suits me fine at the moment. It isn't a place I would pick to live. They come up to Mass with us every day. They will be with us on Christmas Day. We go down to visit them and they come up to us every day.

I was in the nursing home the other day on my way to a meeting and I went in to see this Sarah. She's in the home so I told the three of them here when I came back. I had to take them separately. I said, 'Tess I was in Dublin yesterday to see Sarah and she was asking for you'. I had to call Mary Kate separately and Nell. Why? Because the three of them would be at one another's throats with the jealousy if they saw me telling the others. If you watch out for that kind of thing and be sensitive towards them they are lovely old creatures.

I've been reading a book about the laundry recently. They had a very rough time here. Awful, yes, it sends the shivers up my back at times to think of it. I don't let it in on me really. I wasn't here. I don't know anything about it. I never put a foot in an orphanage in my life. I don't know, I don't know anything about it. You'd be told, honestly, it's what you hear. It was the scene at the time. As I say we had not the luxuries in the fifties that we have now. We say the good old times but they were not good. You can think for yourself now, anyway. You can do what you want. If I feel I can help somebody in any way I'll be glad.

You weren't affirmed in the convent

You'd be amazed at this, I was excellent at art. I never did a bit of it in my early days. I was not asked to do it so I thought I was useless at it and I never bothered doing it. I started last week and I'm enjoying it. What I'm trying to say is you weren't affirmed in the convent, a bit of affirmation would have been good at the time.

I am just beginning to settle here after five years. It's very central here for my family. My nieces and nephews are really lovely to me all the time. I'm busy. I visit a lot. I visit elderly people. Spirituality, faith, prayer life, discipline and good retreats, they help you along. Friends, too, of course, people make it. You make lifelong friendships. But it is with my brother and his wife that I consider home. No matter whether I go to Australia or England or elsewhere for eight years, I'll always come back there to them.

7

Barbara

'A most unnatural way of life'

Introduction

Barbara is seventy-two years of age. She exchanged a warm, loving, and almost idyllic home life for a life of grief and suffering in the convent. Her misery started in primary school when she was slapped by a lay teacher and refused to go to school until her father resolved the issue. She was sent to boarding school at about ten years of age where the nuns also hit her, but she did not tell her parents about this. The cold and damp in the school contrasted with the cosy fires her mother lit in every room in the winter.

When she finished school Barbara wanted to leave Ireland and join a convent in England but was dissuaded by her mother's priest friend. Her only reason for becoming a nun was to become a saint. Barbara had the desire to outdo her mother and father by choosing a way of life that was considered superior. She gives voice to the pre-Vatican II (pre-1962) view that marriage was inferior to religious life and that nuns were spiritually superior. Therefore, in her mind, Barbara had surpassed her parents in her choice of vocation. She had done better. She was also convinced that to leave the convent put one's eternal soul in jeopardy. The Gospel teaches that those who put their hand to the plough and turn back are not worthy to enter the kingdom of heaven. If you enter the convent you go to heaven when you die and you might also become a saint; if you leave you go to hell. Heaven, sainthood and hell are juxtaposed and Barbara made her choice. She links the decision to enter the convent with her decision to remain there. She diminished the parental couple, the 'halfpenny place' they were in, in choosing something superior to a marital relationship. She renounced the idea of a kindly warm family, where she was never struck, for the harsh, cold atmosphere of the convent where she suffered many indignities. She paid a high emotional price for her choice.

Barbara found herself in a double bind when Vatican II removed their special status and nuns were then on a level with their secular counterparts. Nuns were no longer special or superior by virtue of their choice, but it was more difficult to change the second part of the internalised equation. Was hell still the punishment for leaving? She could stay or leave; she opted to stay. She feels wronged and angry by what the Church taught.

By the time she went to university Barbara had internalised the notion that she had no right to make decisions about the money allocated to her. She could not imagine not conforming to what was demanded. Now she is angry, and critical of the system, but she turns her anger in on herself. There are many times when she attacks her own intelligence, and blames herself, calling herself 'stupid' for having believed what she was told. In the light of hindsight, blind obedience and compliance with the rule seems hard to credit. Barbara did not believe she was stupid because she wanted to get an honours degree at university, but she had set her sights on sainthood and was willing to sacrifice all to attain this. Now she is critical of the system and she no longer fears speaking her mind.

Barbara is deeply affected by her thwarted friendship with Father Joe. She cries incessantly as she recalls the story. Barbara's disposition and her flaunting of the rule by having a relationship, however innocent and platonic, infuriates the superior and the system makes her a victim, probably to make an example of her.

The overt reason for the prohibition on dyadic relationships was to avoid sexual encounters between individuals. The less obvious reason was to avoid energy being diverted from the group.[22] *Affective relationships are considered to be a threat to institutional discipline, and if they become too strong, they may bring about the disintegration of the group.*[23] *Members involved in such relationships are likely to be less controllable and less devoted to the exclusive service of the institution.*[24] *So, consistent with the principles of chastity and group coherence, any emotional involvement with another person, inside or outside the convent, has to be avoided.*

Barbara's friend Maria's disposition and valency to be manipulated makes her a suitable candidate to come between Barbara and Father Joe. One could say by Barbara's deeply wounded reaction, forty years after the event, that in her mind, she was engaged to Father Joe. Their relationship was probably innocuous but it represents love, care, intimacy, even sex, all of those things that the sisters renounce through their vow of chastity. Some years later another priest comes to the rescue and initiates Barbara into a spiritual relationship with Jesus, taking Him as her friend. This new relationship, unlike that with Father Joe, will not cause any upset to the system.

While she was still in the novitiate Barbara's mother told her she would always be welcomed at home where there was warmth and care, while the mother superior in the convent takes every opportunity to humiliate and punish her. This is probably partially motivated by the superior's jealousy of Barbara's relationship with Father Joe, and partly her unconscious wish to protect the group integrity and coherence. Barbara praises her mother's bravery and good sense because her mother knew the superior would read her letter. This projection depleted Barbara of her own courage and good sense and she could not bring herself to leave the convent. The superior's command to Barbara to walk down the garden carrying her bedding, in broad daylight, without any explanation, is a metaphor for asking her to leave. Nuns often brought their mattress and bed linen when they entered. Now Barbara was told to remove hers. Years later, the superior admits to her sadism and is clearly bothered by it. Her final coup is to be laid out in Barbara's bed, when she dies, leaving Barbara without anywhere to sleep. The battle has ended.

Life in the convent was so traumatic for Barbara that it has affected her memory and the 'tough life' has destroyed her personality and her initiative. She feels insecure and has never felt supported by superiors. In her present convent there is a 'cold war' situation but 'abuse' such as she experienced in the past would not be tolerated. Throughout her life Barbara moved house several times in an effort to find personal contentment.

Barbara's story represents those who became victims of the system in religious life. Those who defied the rules could not be tolerated and their victimisation served as an example to others. Conformity made life easier to bear. At present, Barbara makes the best of her situation through her concentration on a life of prayer. She is also in a position to spend time on her hobbies.

Barbara's Story:

All the kids in the village played together

There are little things I remember from my childhood in the late 1930s, going along the road for walks with my mother while she pointed out the flowers, my Dad making little toys for us, a cheese box or a butter box with wheels on it. Now the wheels were empty thread reels and there was a bit of twine to pull it around. In the autumn we used to go picking blackberries and there was a dealer buying them to make dye. We used to go out into the fields collecting crab apples and my mother would make crab jelly, and we'd collect mushrooms and there were streams and we'd go fishing, probably with a rush. We didn't have any fancy fishing rods.

All the kids in the village played tag together and in wintertime when there was ice on the road we'd have slides, you see, there were no cars. So we'd have great fun with the slides and we'd go one behind the other, like a train. Sometimes in the summer there used to be open air dancing. Well, we used to dance our legs off, it was great and there'd be crowds of people. They'd all come there on a Sunday. I also remember my first midnight Mass. I thought it was heaven, the beautiful choir and the holly garlands. When we came home my mother had lovely cake and raspberry cordial.

My Dad was a great swimmer. He did everything to teach me how to swim and I'd screech and screech and hold on to him and I wouldn't let go for dear life so he gave up in the end. I absolutely adored him. I used to go cycling with him. I remember one day we cycled thirty-two miles. I just loved being out with him. At night he'd show me all the constellations, the stars and name them for me. I just adored him.

In the morning, we'd walk to school and on the frosty mornings we'd be out in the yard waiting for the school to open because the teacher lived up the road. We'd have great fun, trying to keep ourselves warm, playing games, like jumping to 'ice cream, a penny a lump, the more you eat the more you jump'.

The first time I ever got a slap in my life was in school from a lay teacher, and I remember it reached the stage where I wouldn't go to school. My mother and father never lifted a finger to me in their lives. To be getting slapped was something out of my ken altogether. Eventually, I told my parents and Dad marched down to the teacher and had a chat with her and that was the end of the beatings. Oh, I hated the place. I had a few very good friends there, but you know when you go to boarding school you lose contact with people.

To have nuns slapping you was the pits altogether

So then I went to boarding school. That was a real culture shock to me to find myself in a cold house. There was no central heating or anything and when I got up in the morning my clothes were damp. Now in our house there were fireplaces in all the bedrooms and my mother would have fires lit every single night in the wintertime. It was cosy. You know how cosy it is when you have a fire. So this was an awful shock to me.

Another awful shock I got was to see two nuns having a row. I was gobsmacked. I couldn't believe that nuns would fight. I was in first year and I had no Primary Cert because I wouldn't stay in my old primary school, they would have killed me. I was ten or eleven. The nuns sent me over to the primary school, no preparation or anything but sure I got the old exam anyway. Then they decided it would be a good idea if I did the scholarship the next year. They made all the decisions and they just told my mother. So they sent me over to Augustine, Lord have mercy on her. Oh, she was so cross! God help her she had cancer. I remember seeing her sound asleep at the desk one day. I was afraid of my life of her and of Clare because they were always slapping us. Oh slapped, slapped! You see I wasn't used to it. I used to hear nuns talking about the sally rod that was always on their mantelpiece at home. There was never a sally rod in our house, ever. And then to have nuns slapping you I thought was the pits altogether. I was dying to get back to the secondary school where they wouldn't slap you, although Angela did slap. I think Ignatius slapped too but not much, nothing to gripe about really.

But poor Augustine was so anxious that we would get this scholarship. I believe now it was for her honour and glory because if you didn't get results you were no good as a teacher. But at the time I didn't know that. I thought it was just to make us learn the stuff. We were studying morning, noon and night. So anyway we got the scholarship. We did the scholarship at Easter and I said, 'I'm going back to the secondary school'. I didn't mind secondary school really.

I didn't find secondary school harsh

We had good times. In summertime we'd have picnics down in the bog and in the evening at study time we used to play tennis. It was great. There was no great harshness. I was afraid of Brigid. She had cancer and she would get really angry. She'd fire the book at you, down at your head. But I didn't have her for long. I don't think many of the teachers were qualified. Pauline hadn't a clue and we had Agatha teaching us Art and sure she hadn't a clue about it. When I went into my Leaving Certificate and did my Art the superintendent came down and said, 'Is that the best you can do?' I said, 'I'm afraid it is'.

But the weather, I remember the weather was gorgeous. And we'd go into the chapel on our way to the examination hall and we had no worries about the exam. If we got it well and good, and if we didn't well and good. There was no stress, no pressure good, bad or indifferent. What I hated about the boarding school was getting up early in the morning. Mass was at half seven so we were up at seven. I hated that and I hated the old cold dormitories in the wintertime and washing in cold water, the little hand basin and the jug and showing your nails then to whoever was on duty. We used to love Saturday when we'd go across the road to confessions, just to get out. The walks were really all we had but then the woods were full of hazelnuts and the nuns used to let us into the woods to pick the hazel nuts. That is a lovely memory.

We used to have a Christmas concert and they'd erect a stage with barrels at the bottom of the old study hall and the dressing room was an old cloakroom that would freeze a kitten, and when you came in you had to bend your head to get onto the stage. When I was in first year we got home for Halloween and I was heartbroken coming back. I didn't want to come back but sure I had to. My father wouldn't let me cycle seven or eight miles to the local school in the rain and bad weather. I didn't tell my parents how I felt. I didn't always like boarding school but I couldn't say that it damaged me. You know the way people say, no, I couldn't say it did now because we had good times and then we had fun with our pals.

I have no awful memories of my spiritual year

Funny thing, I wanted to enter in England and Father Tim, my Mam's friend, knew an awful lot of nuns and convents in England; he worked there for years. And he said to my Mam, 'Don't let her next, nigh or near an English convent'. He said they were terrible; sure our own were as bad. I entered then with Geraldine. She was wild and really good fun. We had ten days free and all I remember is she made apple tarts. I hadn't a clue how to make an apple tart.

I spent my spiritual year working in the dining room. You put your foot on a polisher and polished the floor and it kept you nice and trim, that was the way. I have no awful memories of that year. The Novice Mistress wasn't too bad. She wasn't an old toughie; there was a soft side to her. My cousin who was a boarder gave me a banana one day. I handed up the banana to the Novice Mistress and she took it. This will tell you how stupid I was. She probably ate it but I didn't think of that at the time; it's only since, with the passing years it's unreal. She took the banana instead of saying, 'Barbara enjoy it'. A banana, is that stupid or idiotic or naïve? Call it anything you like. That's a hard one to credit.

What I hated was a Saturday morning when the Novice Mistress would examine you on the Catechism of the Vows. We had to learn it by heart. I hated getting up at half five in the morning I needn't tell you, particularly if I was on the call and had to go around knocking on everyone's door saying, 'Benedicamus Domino' (let us praise the Lord). Again I hated the damp rooms because they were damp when we came. We didn't get in the storage heaters until the canon was made parish priest and Teresa told him that there was no heat. She used to tell him everything. He nearly threw a fit and he insisted that we get storage heaters. I don't know how he got away with it. Before that we had no heat at all, the only heat was the fire in the community room and the pipes in the chapel that came out into the little long narrow hall; no hot water, there was one tap down at the toilet on the landing and we used to bring our jugs to get hot water. And by the time we got as far as it the water was cold because it couldn't do the whole crowd of us that were there. So that was the spiritual year. I have no memory of anything extraordinary in that year. It was okay.

I was up in school all day long

So the next year was fine because they put me teaching and I was out of their claws altogether. I was up in school all day long, teaching and no qualifications whatever. Are you listening? And I had the Inter Certs for a few subjects. And they got on grand. You know, I think when you are only half bright you can understand the kids and a bit like my old Maths teacher, drill it into them. That was grand. I was there until March 1958 and then Geraldine and myself made our first profession. I have no memory of anything whatever in that year except teaching. I say to people now that my memory is so bad that I think that it is the trauma of religious life that is to blame. And there are an awful lot of gaps, an awful lot of them, and I really believe it was the tough life. I really do believe that.

We had no pocket money

I went to the university and that was hard in this sense: college wasn't hard, but we were in a hostel, again no heat. It was just a regular house really and we were all on top of one another, all on top of one another and I found that hard, and we had a dining room where we had a table that was only a bench hanging out of a wall going along one side and another one on the other side and a table down the middle. You'd be sitting here with your face to the wall eating your meals. At study you were crowded all on top of one another, the same in the chapel, a little chapel for a crowd of us. All I remember is we were always on top of one another. The only thing was you were young; you couldn't take it if you weren't. We were dying to walk along the prom but we weren't allowed. We were at the seaside – imagine not walking on the prom!

We stayed all day in the university. We used to bring a lunch with us. It was very much convent life. We had no pocket money. If you'd like a bar of chocolate you couldn't go out and buy one. No money at all. You had a certain amount of money for bus fares but you had to write down every single thing and we were so innocent we never wrote down five shillings and got sweets. It would never have entered our heads to buy an apple or a banana or anything. Would you believe that? It just never dawned on me to spend it where I shouldn't spend it. It never dawned on me; I think I was very naïve. I really think I was, I was stupid. But anyway I didn't. I was very honest. There was nothing of the university life, nothing at all, except that in college you would have great fun with the students. So the hostel was just like the convent really.

I used to hate Saturday. I wanted to give up French. The lecturer had an edge on religious and he really used to knock us. I had to go in for lectures on a Saturday. I hadn't time to take my lunch and get in to the lecture on time so I asked the nun in charge if could I have it a little bit earlier but she wouldn't allow it. So I used to have to swallow it down and I used get sick. Apart from that, I had no great problems.

I found it hard enough to get in on the teaching

Then I came home and they put me teaching. I had a pass degree. I wanted to do an honours degree because all my class were doing it but the superior would not let me because I would have three subjects if I did a pass degree. That was stupid because you couldn't teach three subjects and teach them well. But sure you did what you were told and that was it. So I was teaching French to the whole school. After a year I did the Higher Diploma in Dublin. That was a great year. We went out to shows and it was a completely different way of life altogether. I found it hard enough to get in on the teaching when I returned. At that stage I wasn't very fluent. I hadn't had the opportunity of being in the country. I'd been for a month one summer.

Particular friendships were totally condemned

Two things happened. I'm going to cry now at this. I was great friends, as I thought, with Maria and I became good friends with Father Joe. I don't know how but I was very friendly with him. I got friendly with him during holiday time when I came home from college and they put me on the parlours to serve the breakfasts, teas and dinners. He was just about a year or two ordained; he was very young. He is three years older than I am. I remember serving him his breakfast. I didn't have much time. I'd have a few words with him, standing, before I'd run off. He had a freedom we didn't have. He'd phone me and you'd be terrified to take a phone call in those days. We only met if I was out for a walk. Particular friendships were totally condemned. The superiors had an awful set on nuns who were friends. Anywhere there was a friendship it was absolutely, totally condemned.

I think you weren't meant to have feelings. But I certainly had feelings when Father Joe came on the scene and Maria would have known that. I thought she was my best friend and we'd go out for walks and I'd often bring her in to see him for a chat. I would never go on my own. He would give me chocolates and I'd share them with her and he'd give me money to go to the pictures and I'd always share it with her. Now I often wondered, because he was so good-humoured and so nice, if she would have loved to be his friend, and I could understand that, but what I couldn't understand is what she did to me.

It was early 1969 and I was out at the dentist. Maria was server at lunch and we used to wear white aprons and sleeves when we were serving in the refectory. I came in and the sisters had gone out of the refectory, saying the Miserere, and Maria was eating her dinner. I went to the hatch to get my dinner and Maria came down to me and said, 'Father Joe was up to see me and he said to tell you the engagement is off'.

I was speechless. I said, 'What?'

'He said to tell you the engagement was off.'

Various things happened after that. She was portress, answering the hall door and the phone. We'd come in to the chapel for night prayer and she'd say to me, 'Father Joe was on the phone and he said to tell you he was asking for you'. I couldn't figure it out. So anyway, to make a long story short, he did try to make it up with me and I used to talk to him but I had lost trust completely. I struggled with that for a long time. I couldn't figure out why he had come up to her, what she had said, or what he had said.

Later, I heard that she had sent for him so when I met him I asked, 'Is it true that Maria sent for you that day?' Well he criticised her but that didn't wash with me at all because he should have stood on his own two feet. She made him promise that he would never reveal to me what she had said to him. So I struggled with that, I had lost trust completely and I'm still struggling with it. I couldn't tell you what it did to me. I trusted nobody.

Months later, when I was doing a Holy Hour, and just as the hour was over, on the dot of the hour there was a ring at the hall door and I opened it and it was Maria. 'Good God,' I said and 'What's this?' I brought her in and had a cup of tea and while she was there I said to her that I was working on the healing of memories and that I'd like her to help me. I said, 'Do you remember this and this and this?'

'Now that you have mentioned it to me I know I will remember.'

'If you do, would you ever talk to me about it?'

So then at my next session with my counsellor I said, 'I don't believe her. If I did that to a person I would remember, such an ugly thing.'

'Now you are being judgemental. When we do ugly things we sometimes block them out, maybe she has blocked it out.'

'I don't believe it, I really don't believe it.'

Later I met Maria and I asked, 'Maria now that we are here, do you remember a few years back?'

'Oh yeah, yeah, were you having problems with Father Joe?'

'Not at all. I wasn't having problems with him, sure we scarcely ever saw one another. What I don't understand, what I found really hurtful, was that you told me he came up to see you but you didn't tell me you sent for him.'

'I don't remember sending for him.'

'The girl you sent to get him told me and he himself told me.'

'Well, if two people told you it must be true. Well, anyway, there was no malice in it.'

She apologised to me there and then. But I couldn't tell you what it did to me. I thought she was my friend and he was my friend. I have tried to suppress my anger with her. I brought her the most beautiful gifts from America. I thought that I was coming to terms with it. But obviously it wasn't the case. I will say this. When I was very friendly with her I couldn't turn on my ankle but she was there. I found her very clingy. I didn't like that. I liked my space. I like to be friends but I like space. But even with all of that I was devastated with what she did. I didn't want to carry her on my shoulders. I didn't want to bear a grudge towards her. The shutters just came down. Her awful betrayal was the thing that had the biggest effect on me, and I still cannot know what it was about.

Then I couldn't stop crying

And then shortly after that Daddy died. That was the pits altogether. I'll never forget that. I absolutely adored him. I just loved being out with him. He died and my mother had a breakdown. So that was tough, oh, that was tough. Why am I telling you that? I'll tell you what I found hard. I still had to continue supervising study and getting the kids up in the morning even though my mother was ill. There was no help. No one said, 'Barbara, you can be off study or you needn't put them to bed'. There was no help and I remember at that time Joan saying I wasn't pulling my weight. I couldn't pull any more. Mammy folded up when Daddy died. Then I couldn't stop crying. I was crying everywhere and I went to poor Patrick and I said, 'I can't stop crying and I don't know why'. But sure it was Daddy. But God help her she gave me a bottle of Buckfast wine.

The way to sainthood

Superiors were hard. If you take how Benedict treated me. She was allergic to me; she broke out in a rash when she saw me. I was in the parlour one day with a crowd of the nuns and Father Joe was there and we were having great fun, and Benedict sent for me and told me I was to leave the parlour. I wasn't to be in there with Father Joe. She didn't put anybody else out but she put me out.

When I was a white veil I used to clean the parish church on a Saturday. A couple of us used to do it. And when it came to Christmas, the canon, as a treat, brought the cleaners out to see the Christmas lights in the town and then down to a branch house to get a nice tea. Benedict wouldn't let me go.

I fell asleep one morning in the chapel at meditation and she put me out in the garden for meditation every morning for weeks after that. It was winter and it was dark and I was scared out of my wits, out in the garden at that hour of the morning. I couldn't stay awake at my prayers so I had to go to the garden for meditation at half five in the morning. I was terrified. I was probably only a white veil or a novice or something. She was superior. The Novice Mistress had no say, no say whatever. She had to go to Benedict for everything.

One day, at recreation time, I had the kids for recreation. I was talking to two of them and she came up, with arms akimbo. She called me and she brought me around by the tennis court. I was in charge of the games and fortunately there was a basketball ring broken. So she read me for that and she read me for talking to the two girls and when I went back they said, 'Sister, did she give out to you?' and I said that she was pointing out the broken basketball ring, which was half the truth but at least I didn't have to tell them a lie.

I was sleeping in the boarding school with another nun. We were in charge of the boarders so we slept upstairs in a cell. We were very naïve. I can tell you honestly when we went inside that door we never broke silence. You can believe that or not but that is true. One morning I was in class and Benedict sent for me. She said, 'You are to bring your mattress and your bedclothes down to the convent'. Another nun was sent up instead of me. I don't know what that was about but I was ashamed of my life coming down the garden in the middle of class with my mattress and my blankets.

I had my mind made up to leave the convent and I said, 'That lady won't always be superior and why should I throw away all I believe in'. Stupidly, I still believed this life would get you on the road to sainthood. I really did think it was the way to saint-hood and I thought that my mother and father and all those who got married were in the halfpenny place. I thought that priests and religious were way up there. Not up there in the sense that I would look down on anybody, but that in the spiritual life we were away up there. Yes, I did, and then another wrong, a misun-derstanding, whatever you like to call it, is that line in the Gos-pel, 'Put your hands to the plough and turn back and you're not fit to enter the kingdom of heaven'. Now that was drilled into us.

Shortly after I entered my mother wrote and told me I was never to hesitate if I wanted to come home, that I'd be very wel-come home if I didn't want to stay or if I thought the life wasn't for me. Funnily enough, I knew our letters were read; my mother knew our letters were read. I said to myself later, brave woman! She wrote that to me so, from the point of view of family, I would have had no problem if I left. So I was fortunate in that my moth-er had good sense.

I remember one evening at supper we were allowed to speak and it was the big long tables and I happened to be opposite

Benedict. I don't know what she was talking about but she was saying how nervous she was about dying and I said, 'Sure Mother, what would you be afraid of dying for? For God's sake, you gave your whole life in religion, what would you be afraid of?'

She turned to me and she said, 'It's all right for you to talk but you never deliberately set out to hurt somebody'.

Three weeks before she got sick and died she met Olive and she said to her, 'Were you Sister Barbara's Novice Mistress?'

Poor Olive nearly died because she knew the set Benedict had on me, and she thought, what's coming now? And she said, 'I was, Mother'.

'Well,' she said, 'I'm terribly sorry for the way I treated her.'

I was sleeping in the infirmary. I was in the infirmary for years because there was no place; there was no bed for me. And there was a knock at my door at three o'clock in the morning. 'Come out, Benedict is dying.'

So I came out and we said the prayers and she died and then she was laid out in my bed in the infirmary and I had no bed to get into. Well, the others screeched, they said, 'Barbara, she had you in life and she got you in death'. She had an incredible set on me.

You were supposed to be a doormat

I would say there was a lot of injustice, an awful lot of injustice. The more the superiors came down on you the better it was. You were supposed to be the mat. You know Rodriquez, you had to plant cabbages upside down and you went out and you planted them upside down as if they were going to grow and silly things like that, pure obedience, blind obedience, and you were supposed to be a doormat where people could walk across you. But it didn't apply to the authorities. If they went away they would come back and have their tea in the parlour, sweet cake and biscuits and what have you. People put up with it. Why? I have asked that question a thousand times and people say, 'Barbara, get off your hobby horse'. People would say to me that if you opened your mouth you got the door. Sent home. Yes, that's what they said to me because I have asked this question a hundred thousand times. But I stayed myself in spite of all of that, you know. But I knew that if I went home I was all right. I would be accepted. At least I had that.

Even now most people would be very insecure and they would find it very hard to leave, to take that step, because we were never allowed to do anything. So how would you manage? I would say there would be a lot of insecurity from that point of view. You became helpless. Then you couldn't do anything. Until we got into regular clothes and could move out and got cars it was regulated from morning till night, every minute was regulated.

Round the time of Benedict's death was the first retreat we made with Father John and he made religion and our relationship with Jesus so real that, that it was my turning point where prayer was concerned. I got away from reading books and began to be able to talk to Jesus, as my friend. Now I have to thank John for that. I also had a wonderful escape in a family who were my friends and lived nearby. I'd shoot down there and have tea in the evenings. They were so near it was very easy to skip down. That was a great release. Also I loved the teaching. I'd go up to school on a Saturday and a Sunday and I'd be up there all day, preparing my work and I suppose I thought I was being really conscientious, getting my classes ready, and I was really, but I think it was an escape from down below at the same time.

Would you go to the small house?

So then the years went by and there was talk of going into small houses. I hadn't a clue how to cook and I was an awful eejit too. I went down to the provincial one day and I said:

'Could I do a Home Economics course somewhere so that if I go into a small house I'll be able to do my bit the same as everybody else.'

'I'll certainly get you to do the course but you're the first person who has come into my head for this, would you go to the small house we are opening?'

'I will of course, if you want me to. I've no problem with that. I will if you think I'll be okay there.'

She warned me I wasn't to tell a person, I was the first person on her list. Then we had a meeting and everybody who was interested went to it.

Later the provincial called me on the phone and said, 'A, B and C are going to the small house. You're not going this time, better luck next time.'

So she came then for visitation and she was at dinner and she put the list down at the bottom of the dining room with the times for people to go in to her. I didn't put down my name and I was down washing my dishes and she said, 'I don't see your name down here, Barbara.'

'No, I'm not putting it down.'

'Are you not coming in? It's visitation, come in and talk to me.'

'I've nothing to say to you.'

'Well, I think you should have something to say to your Mother General.'

'If you want me to go in I'll go in.'

This is so stupid! She was in the parlour sitting at one end so I sat down at the back wall. Then I told her what I thought, that what she had done was despicable and she said, 'You wouldn't be fit to live in a small community'.

I thought I was going to get a nervous breakdown

I went out to America for a holiday and the parish priest asked me if I'd stay for a year. Even though I wasn't a grade school teacher I did it. Then he asked me if I would do another year and another year. So then, at fifty-nine years old, I said, 'I'll have to come back on account of my pension'. So I came back to the house where I was appointed and the welcome!

Monica said, 'There are plenty of rooms empty up the road, why weren't you sent up there?' They were the words. That's the welcome I got. I was home to teach for the year. The school was hard enough without this. Everybody in this house was upset, I saw two of the nuns crying and all they wanted was a bit of peace. Margaret was sent to this house and it was grand for a while, and then the trouble started and she called headquarters one day and said, 'If you don't do something I'm going to commit suicide, I can't stand it'. I don't know what wheels they set in motion but anyway they gave her six hundred Euro for, what do you call it, disturbance money! At the end of that year I thought I was going to get a nervous breakdown so I took early retirement without asking anybody and I wrote to the provincial team and said I wanted a sabbatical. Then I went away for the year.

None of their sisters would go into the house

Then I was asked if I would go to a small house that needed leaders. I had no reason not to go. Another sister, Anne, was sent as well. We became great friends and she is a real outgoing person, full of fun and good humour, a lovely person. So we went together for the few years. The provincial team never told us anything about the difficulties there and that none of their own sisters would go into the house. It was a very, very, very difficult house. Anyway, we hammered along together. The provincial team didn't give us any support really, and not only that but they wanted to send in this sister from another order who needed accommodation. We were terrified because there was a sister in the house who was a kleptomaniac and if the visitor had put her food into the press or the fridge it would be gone. You could leave nothing out of your hands or it would be gone. We had to lock our doors and everything. The poor creature, God help her, she'd take the eye out of your head.

We had a great three years. I think it was mainly due to my companion. You know she was such a lovely, lovely, lovely person and she was awfully funny. She would see the funny side of everything and she said her mother used to always tell her if there was a problem to look at the funny side and she had a gift for doing that and she was just lovely. Then the house was due to close. The reason I came back here was I thought there was such demand on places here that I wouldn't get inside the door. So that brings me up to here.

I have huge questions over religious life

If we bring it around to the present it's not great now. When you are teaching you have an outside interest but that's gone now. Our present leader is like a dog with a bone; when she gets an idea, that's it. She'll see that through no matter what. I took on some jobs here but when I went away she brought in lay staff to do them. She never told me she was going to do it. She never told me she had done it. No more than if it was of no consequence whatever she never mentioned it to me. It was the staff who told me that they were doing it. I'd lost my job, and there was no more regard on it than if you were just a fly on the wall and that's the way. She'll use you as long as you are useful but I was really shaken that she would do it without even telling me.

I feel if I start confronting and challenging her I will lose my peace of mind and then when I go to prayer I will be complaining about her in my mind, and I will end up in chaos. I think for a lot of people that the fight is gone out of them. They are just gone beyond the age when they want to fight for their rights. That's where we are now, so I have huge question marks over religious life, huge. I think at this stage the fight is gone. You know you want to live in peace. Now you'll say peace at all costs. It's a repeat of the past except that she couldn't abuse me the way Benedict could. Do you know she can't do that? It's a very cold war kind of thing. People are very restless so I think that the provincial will put in a team in charge here instead of having one leader, but no one wants the job because any bit of personality we had was beaten out of us in the past. It was beaten out of us.

The few years that Anne and I were in charge in the small house really went a bomb. They love to see me coming back and I know that and it's genuine. But I would attribute that to Anne. She's just beautiful and it was so easy to work with her. There were only four old sisters and the two of us. This convent is different because it is huge. I would never have felt adequate to being in charge here. But I do think that any initiative we had was beaten out of us. We became helpless really. It was a very harsh way of life.

When I think that there were four of us sleeping up in the laundry and the ivy and the mould on the walls. I mean, if we put that in a book today! If the orphans were put sleeping in it could you imagine the outcry. If we rang a certain radio programme, I mean, imagine it! And yet they felt it was all right to do that to us. There was no space because they had taken in more people than they could accommodate. It was outrageous. The ivy, now I'm not exaggerating, the ivy was coming down the walls and the blue mould or whatever kind of mould and all the plaster falling off. There were older people than me there. It wasn't the four last juniors who were put into it. No heat, no nothing, the outer room of the laundry, underground. Later we got rooms.

You know, it was a very harsh regime. I have come across the lack of care in story after story from sisters I have lived with and worked with and met in college. You see, there was no opportunity for showing compassion because you couldn't speak except for the half hour of recreation. You were meant to be silent all the time except for that half hour. You didn't speak to the people you met in the garden. You didn't speak to the children. You didn't speak except maybe for the twenty minutes teachers' break you had in the staff room, do you see?

As I already said, in the past particular friendships were forbidden because of a fear of lesbianism but they never put words on it. It was from Father Joe that I learned what lesbianism was. The nuns' femininity and maternity were denied. Someone said, 'neuter gender', neuter gender absolutely. Now there's more room for feelings and emotions and that kind of thing, certainly there is. I would say people lead a more normal life. We are not living in fear, you know, the fear of talking when you shouldn't be talking or making noise when you shouldn't be making noise or breaking a plate. There was an awful lot of fear in the past. There really was, when you think of it. The harshness and the injustice and the lack of charity and the jealousy and the envy and the putting down when it was supposed to be loving one another and helping one another and helping children. There was a cruelty that rolled over on to the children because if you are not happy within yourself it is going to come out on the children. I suppose I compensated because I loved teaching. Once I started teaching I loved it, I absolutely loved it, so I don't think I was hard on the kids in school. I don't think I was. We were always told we couldn't give what we haven't got, so if we haven't got love and charity in our lives and we walk into the classroom, we can't give it.

There are a lot of things I forget. When I hear some of the others reminiscing I have it all forgotten. I find it upsetting. It's only lately I began thinking about it. When I began thinking about religious life and the way it developed, the harshness, when I began to realise that it was such a harsh life. 'Gosh,' I said, 'It must have been that that knocked my memory, knocked things out of my head.' And I suppose I became very aware of it when that counsellor told me that you could block things out of your life. You see, I couldn't imagine blocking things out of my life. I imagined they are all there in the memory. Oh yes, I'd have fierce questions about the life.

What I can say to you is that the spiritual means more to me now than it ever did and I have time. I love adoration of the Blessed Sacrament and I find it easier to focus when I have the Blessed Sacrament there. Now in retirement I have so much more time to reflect, to pray, and when I say to pray it's not rattling off prayers. The time I spend in prayer is an absolute luxury. As well as that, I can use my leisure time to follow my untapped talents. That's a gift we can avail of now.

Religious life will fizzle out. I wouldn't encourage anybody to enter. Now I'm being honest with you, I wouldn't encourage anybody. I think it's a very unnatural way of life. I really think it's an unnatural way of life.

8

Clare

'We're paddling and we're drowning'

Introduction

Clare comes from a large family. She is now seventy-two years of age. Her parents had an excellent relationship. The children engaged in play together. Everything was discussed in the house and this openness had to be curbed outside the home, in school and later in the convent. On the other hand, Clare had a fairly strict upbringing. She was not free to walk the town or go to a dance until after her Leaving Cert.

Clare's decision to become a nun was measured and she struggled with it, although initially it stemmed from sibling rivalry. Her reaction to her brother's decision to enter the priesthood prompted her to become a nun. She prayed a lot about it. At her first dance, in spite of the novelty and excitement, she thought there had to be something more to life. Finally, having talked to a priest and the school principal she made her decision. Clare's mother rejoiced; nothing could have been better than to have had a priest and a nun in the family. Her father did not speak much about it. Clare's parents' reactions represent the two sides of the coin, the joy and status of having a nun in the family and the loss of your daughter and her potential family. In Irish society, at the time, having a son who was a priest and a daughter a nun bestowed respectability of the highest order.

Clare could see the roof of her house from the convent but was not allowed to go home. She found the silence and required religious decorum of the convent very difficult and felt she did not 'fit the mould'. Kicking stones down the drive in anger and frustration at the locked gate certainly did not fit the mould. However she threw herself with abandonment into the life and strove to be perfect. Later, she modified this ideal but she always remained committed to the demands of convent life.

When her older sister died in England Clare was not even allowed to visit her home, ten minutes away. Reflecting on this she wonders why the nuns accepted the unnatural rules and the regimentation that thwarted her psychological growth at eighteen years of age. She has no answer. Acceptance was part of the culture of the time. Later, when she speaks of her duties, teaching, taking study and cleaning the school, she says she took it all for granted. Settling down in the convent meant accepting without question what one found to be the norm, in other words, becoming institutionalised. A further example of this is that when Clare entered she could not help speaking her mind, but she soon learned that this was not acceptable so she tried to conform. She suggests that those who left their teaching positions after Vatican II to follow other professions such as alternative therapies and counselling may be on a search for personal fulfilment, trying to repair the damage of their early lives.

She believes that her surgery was as a result of a 'backlog' of suppressed anger and she attributes illness, in the past, to suppressed feelings. The nuns' illness benefitted the doctors and hospitals as nuns sought respite and comfort. Clare's insight is retrospective and, unfortunately, there was no one, at the time, to hear the nuns' cries for help. Life was very difficult at this time, and there was little that the sisters could do against the system. Illness was the only legitimate way the nuns had of getting in touch with their bodies. The harsh life had to be endured until the change came.

Clare's response to the question of the lay sisters in her convent is somewhat confused. They 'resented' their lowly position as cooks and dairymaids as well as doing the laundry and helping the nurse with the sick. Clare sees some of them, not as servants, but as 'really great saints'. She may feel some guilt about their position but buries her feelings by promoting their reward in the next life to the highest rank.

A period in leadership during the transition period after Vatican II left Clare disillusioned with the nuns' commitment to the life. While most nuns threw themselves with enthusiasm into their newfound freedoms and the shedding of outmoded devotional practices, they had little time for developing spirituality. She laughs as she tells of nuns being taught by Father James how to talk 'one at a time' and how to hold meetings. The nuns were being offered the chance to speak but, until now, they had lived silent, enclosed and very restricted lives where no one was interested in what they had to say, so teaching them how to speak at meetings was not very productive. She says some were not mature. They first needed to be helped to think, not just to have thoughts and ideas. Clare's laughter is probably a defence against her embarrassment at the ineptitude of these adult women and the sadness at their plight. She knows that what was provided to adapt to change was inadequate.

She seeks to balance the gains and the losses. She is conflicted. She sees that the structural configuration of the past, with its hierarchical arrangement, afforded stability and holding, but she is unsure about the deference demanded by seniority, 'respected or *kowtowed to'? This uncertainty betrays her ambivalence towards the past. Was it a system that demanded servility, or were people motivated by esteem for their seniors? She is not sure. There is a tension between the past and the present. However the certainty of knowing where one stood in the past was reassuring to her and the system ran smoothly.*

The right to have one's say has led to strong personalities who may suffer from personality disorders, or are unsuited to religious life, creating problems for everyone. In Clare's experience no one was ever sent away. Acting as an individual may be a right but it may have consequences for the group. She is concerned about the conflict between personal freedoms and the institutional mission as she sees a laissez-faire attitude towards the greater good develop and institutional projects enthusiastically begun and later abandoned.

She raises the question of abuse and tries to respond to everyone's dilemma about the 'others'; why did they stand by and do nothing? She knows that the 'others' would not be listened to in the past and they might be ostracised if they complained about things such as the treatment of children. Clare finds herself in a similar position at present. If she spoke her truth at chapter about things such as abandoned projects or living singly without chapter approval she feels she would be 'bombed' out of it. Nothing has changed in that regard.

She is aware that nuns took out their anger and rage on subordinates and tells a story to illustrate the point. On reflection she is amazed at what the nuns tolerated in the past and she is empathic towards the elderly while acknowledging the difficulties of living with them. She is disheartened by the present situation of religious life as she tries to make decisions for her future.

Clare is a thinker and she is the only one of the group who has attempted to get an overview of the entire system of religious life. She is and always was committed to leading a spiritual life although she took rather extreme measures to do this initially. In trying to balance the losses and gains of religious life since Vatican II she becomes confused and has no ally to help her think it through. As a child she tried to revive the dead fish, now she thinks of reviving religious life. She would like the pendulum to swing back a little. She dreams of new beginnings, a fresh start.

Clare's Story:

We were a very open group

In my early days we were out playing house in an old set of houses that had fallen into disrepair. We hated when we were called in, in the evening. We went out to streams and rivers catching fish, little sprats, selling them to each other and exchanging them. Mine always seemed to die. I spent my life trying to re-float them and thinking if I put them on the top of the water often enough they'd really come back to life but it never worked.

I am one of a family of ten. I was the youngest girl and there were two boys younger than me. I grew up in an extremely happy home. My father was very quiet, laid back. Mammy was the goer. I suppose she was the boss but there was a tremendous relationship between them and that permeated through the family. We were a very open group, everything was talked about and we were all there together and we played together. Mammy was a very prayerful person and I can remember a picture of the Sacred Heart in the kitchen and she stopping and looking up at it. I didn't know what she was doing at the time.

I was in the band

I was in the band in first class. We played at break time every day. The entire band gathered and all the classes marched out and we stood there in the corridor and played. That was big. When it came to writing I didn't score too well with that same sister because we had to 'keep between the blue lines', and at times I would get so nervous that my hand would jerk and I would go below the line so I got slapped. I didn't like that.

When I was making my first Communion the sister who prepared us had the very strong message that Jesus would be living in us. The day of my first Holy Communion, with the excitement it must have been about two o'clock, and it suddenly dawned on me that Jesus was in me and I had never thought of it and he had got nothing to eat. So I went to the kitchen press and I took out a slice of bread, took pieces out of it, put it in my mouth and swallowed it and with each swallow I said, 'Now Jesus, that's for you'.

Very early on in my school life I began to notice distinctions between people. The fact was that the well off would be treated in a slightly different way to the less well off, and I came into the latter category. With ten of us at home we were basically all right but we didn't have any of the extras or the luxuries. I was aware of that and I remember one awfully nice experience with one of the sisters who taught me. I used to bring a bottle of milk or tea or cocoa to school and there was a huge open fire in the classroom and the bottles were put around it in a semi-circle, and the girl who was looking after them was a go ahead person and I had noticed that my poor bottle was always at the back so it was always cold. One day the nun was watching when I handed the girl my bottle and she put it in its usual place and the nun just stepped down and took it and put it in the front. Ah, I loved her, I loved her forever. I don't know why I noticed it. It wouldn't have been something that would have been talked about at home or anything like that but I was aware of it.

I started singing out loud

I got on fine in school and I was never in any bother except in sixth class one day I started singing out loud in class. Well the nun nearly fainted, 'What do you mean?' she said. 'What did you do that for?' and I had no answer. It was just a spontaneous outbreak of singing. I got into the same trouble in the novitiate later on for the same thing, but I suppose I was just content and happy in myself. I loved school. During that time life went on at home and we always had great fun. I was very close to my father, very, very close to him as a child and growing up, and there was a great old bond between us. Then I went on to secondary.

Life in the secondary school was really good. We did plays and I'd be in them and I enjoyed it although I'd be quite nervous. Then at sixth year level I began to get a *biteen* moody, everything was getting a bit boring for me. I was growing up and I spent hours looking at myself in the mirror and combing my hair and wondering could I get this or could I get that. There was no going wild or getting to a dance, no way, until I did my Leaving Cert. Even though I had older brothers and sisters there was no way. In fact, my mother would never let me go down town twice the one evening. She said, 'Oh if you are seen walking the street you'll get a very bad name', so she would do without a message rather than let me down twice. Oh yes, she was particular that way. All through my secondary school I went to morning Mass. My mother went and my father went when he retired. It was just a normal thing. I got up at eight, went to Mass, came home had breakfast and went to school.

I was let go to the dance

I began to think a lot about entering. I had a brother who went on for the priesthood and the day he went I said to myself, 'Well if he is going to be a priest I'm going to be a nun'. Then, as a big concession the July before my results came out, I was let go to the dance. I got a new dress and new high heels and I was in heaven. When you are the youngest of four girls it is mostly hand-me-downs but here I was with my very own new dress and I thought it was heaven on earth. I was only home from that dance when I was on for the next one. But it would strike me in the middle of the dance, is this all there is to life, is this all there is to it? Even though I was bursting to go to the dance and I enjoyed it when it was over there was always that sense that there must be more, there has to be something more in life. So I battled with that for a while. I spoke to the usual priests at retreats and the principal of the school. She was very nice, very good, because she didn't say to me, won't you come with us and I'm sure it was something she would have wanted but she left it totally open. I always appreciated that. I had prayed a lot about it.

A son a priest and a daughter a nun

I made the decision. My mother was delighted. She was going to have a son who was a priest and a daughter a nun; that was as good as you would get. My father didn't say anything. He was quiet about it all. He didn't talk much about it. He let Mammy get on with the preparations. None of the family would come with me the day I was entering except my mother and my brother who was ordained at the time. It's amazing how busy they all got that day. When the dinner was over I was inside in the sitting room putting my pieces together and my poor old father came in and said to me, 'If you're not happy come home to us'. It was as much as he was able to say but it said everything. In actual fact, I never got home in his lifetime. He had died before I got home. He was heartbroken. It was years later before I realised how much it had taken out of him and Mammy. I was so taken up with my life and what I was doing that I didn't really appreciate what they were going through. That came later when they'd visit. The regulation was one hour once a month, which was quite strict. My father would say, 'When will you be able to come down home?' I was ten minutes from home. I could see the roof of my house from the convent. I would never advise anyone to enter in her home town.

They sent me to the primary school

I entered on a Wednesday. We got a lovely tea with buns and cakes. I thought it was great. I remember the older nuns saying to me, 'Eat plenty now because you won't be getting them every day'. I didn't take much heed of this. I was disgusted that the next day they made me go to school. Four had entered the previous August. They sent me to the primary school the next day and I was disgusted. I thought at least they'd give me a few days to find my way around, but no, I went to school. I was helping out. I began to realise the week was great when you were in school and then I used to find Saturday and Sunday very long. I went every day from the day I came in and I got no pay either. I was thinking, now less would do ye. Ye could have given me a day or two. I wouldn't have voiced it of course. The five of us had good old fun. Getting up early in the morning was hard. We were up at six, down in the chapel at half six for Mass at half seven. But I was quite happy.

The postulancy was hard in ways. I would have thought, even then, it was hard on a young person starting out. Everything was regulated. There wasn't much room for creativity. One of the community said to me, 'They'll never manage to get you into the mould, you just won't fit in'. I'd say that was a hard part of my life, that mould thing. I didn't fit the mould. Then I was teaching in the school. I wasn't received until January so I was a postulant for eleven months. Now the Novice Mistress told me that had I been a good postulant I would have been received at six months. I didn't believe it, but she said it.

Abandonment to Divine Providence

So when the eleven months were up they couldn't blessed well hold me any longer! The real reason I was held back was because they were holding a job for somebody. I was received and I went on my spiritual year but I got awful holy in that year. Ah gee, St Paul had nothing on me for keeping the rule. I kept it, I was so good, I tried to do everything right and even the Novice Mistress I had after my first profession said to me, 'You know even when you do something wrong you make a good job of it'. To me it was serious business. I was there and I was going to give the hundred per cent.

During the spiritual year I was given a book to follow. *Abandonment to Divine Providence* was the title. I took it very seriously. In my second year as a white veil visits from home resumed. I think I only had one every three months on my spiritual year. I was becoming detached from all worldly matters. When Mammy and Daddy came I refrained from asking about home, I was just so good. One day Mammy came up and she said, 'We got a new press into the kitchen'. Oh God, I forgot all about my abandonment to Divine Providence and I began quizzing her, 'Where did you put this and where did you put that?' The hour flew by and they said good-bye and they went out. Mammy sneaked back and she said. 'Oh, Thank God, you're yourself, you were awful queer for the last while'. So much for my efforts at sanctity! But I took it quite seriously. My mother noticed I was different but I wasn't aware of it. She was worried. She thought there was something terrible happening to me. I was delighted that I had succeeded. I hadn't asked my parents any questions. I was really moving on to sainthood fast! I think that is where I tried to cut out anything that I thought that God mightn't have wanted. I cannot say it lasted. How long did it last? I don't know, but I do know that I tried to do everything as perfectly as I could.

I gave it one hundred and ten per cent

Then came first profession and fortunately for me there was a change of Novice Mistress. The new one was a lot more human. She was a lot more tolerant of young people. I found it so much easier. The first Novice Mistress died over in the nursing home some years ago and one day that I was over visiting her and she just looked at me and said, 'I was very hard on you', and I said in my own mind, you can say that. She was. I think I was totally spontaneous. If a thought came into my head I verbalised it and I suppose coming from my family, where there were ten of us, there was the rough and tumble. You said things, you did things, you let go of things but it took me a long time, a very long time, to learn that in religious life you couldn't do that. If I thought something wasn't right I'd say it and I could never understand why people would got so angry when you said something wasn't right. I mean, if it wasn't right, it wasn't right. I found those two years up to my profession tough. I was aware of a certain pressure in my life. I had this ideal; I was trying to be perfect. I gave one hundred and ten per cent all my life no matter what job I had to do. I really did.

Growth was cut off

So then I went to do the degree. Ah gee, that was heaven. I just loved it, four years of bliss. I suppose after the novitiate years, just to be out! Mind you, life was very confined, we weren't allowed to go in or out of the city, but it was great. There was great camaraderie. There was a big crowd of us there in the hostel. We had great fun and I loved study. I just loved it. I never got tired of it. Oh, it was heaven that went on for four years.

During that time my sister died of cancer. She died in England. She was a young married woman at the time so that was a huge blow. In those days I wasn't allowed home. There was no question of going to England and I wasn't allowed home either.

That was very, very tough and you know you look back at it and you say, 'What was wrong with us, we all had some intelligence why did we accept these things?' We did. I would say, in retrospect, I came in at eighteen, not fully matured, and whatever stage my growth was at then, it was cut off. It was cut off there. There was no growth after that. There was regimentation after that and that's probably why it was difficult.

There was a lot of it that wasn't natural, even though every rule I was supposed to keep I kept. I really did, even down to the particular examen. I'd spend the quarter of an hour in the chapel and I could never figure out what I had taken as a subject (humility, conformity to the will of God, charity etc.). Then infringing the silence was such an awful sin and I couldn't keep my mouth shut. I was always talking so that was something I got a lot of flack over.

They resented being lay sisters

We had the lay sisters when I entered first. They weren't sent away for training. They hadn't secondary education. When I was entering there was no dowry. You had to bring the bed, the jug, the basin and the blankets but there was no dowry, there was no money exchanged. Professing sisters as lay sisters ended around the seventies. They became community sisters then. They resented being lay sisters. They worked in the kitchen and they did the cooking and the laundry and helped the nurses with the sick. They did the dairy, the milk and the butter and the cattle and all that. A lot of these were really great saints, no doubt about it.

There were only four of us

But anyway, I did the degree and the Higher Diploma and I was sent off on my first assignment. The next morning I got word to go to a different school. A new school had just opened and they wanted a Maths teacher. I had never taught Maths but my brother, the priest, was a Maths teacher. They decided if he was able to teach Maths I would be bound to be able to teach it. The poor fellow came down every single Friday to prepare my week's Maths with me. It was a small school and there were four nuns and one lay teacher. We lived in a house. You know, it was grand, right in the centre of the town. The key was always in the front door. We never took it out until we were going to bed at night. It was that kind of time. We went down to the church to Mass in the morning and we came back and we taught our day, and we supervised study in the evenings because the students had to wait until seven-thirty for the ordinary bus service. On a Saturday we had to clean the school. The principal did the books and the secretarial work. We cleaned all the classrooms. It was hard, hard work. We taught on Saturday as well, until one o'clock. I took it all for granted. We taught all the subjects through Irish in those days. It was hard but it was good. Life at community level wasn't particularly easy because there were two who made life difficult for others, watching, assuming and criticising. There's a certain stress attached to that kind of thing. I was six years there.

My father died in that last year. He used to always talk about being afraid of dying and he said, 'If you are with me I won't be afraid', and I said, 'Well, fair enough', and I didn't know how that could happen. I was in class and I got a call that Daddy had got a very bad turn. A priest who was teaching with us brought me to the hospital and I stayed there. I was with him and he'd be in a kind of sleep and if he woke up he asked, 'Where is she?' If I were there he was grand, if not he'd ask, 'Where is she?' So it was great that I was with him at the very end. I had never got home while he was alive so I felt I had missed out on that. But I was really grateful to God that I was with him when he died. So my mother was on her own then and the superiors decided they'd let me live near her. At that stage the rest of my family had moved away.

Forty-five in community

So I went back into the community again and there was a huge crowd of nuns there, about forty-five in all. I was one of the younger nuns. My mother was alone and she found it very difficult to cope without my father. I started to go home and I suppose that was big mistake. I was exhausted. My mother was dependent on me and I was trying to live my own religious life. There was so much expected of me because I was one of the young nuns.

In those days we were doing night duty in the convent as well. We had older sisters and we had to get up to get them out to the loo at night and we did that for thirteen consecutive years. We did that and we went to school the next day and we were let go to bed at seven o'clock the next evening. We got a fry for supper but that was it. I was still being a very good girl, keeping all the rules and the regulations, tearing my hair out with frustration.

We had a lot of sick, elderly in the convent. You brought up a cup of hot milk at four o'clock and you filled their jars and you brought up breakfast in the morning and their tea in the evening. Looking back, I think that a lot of these old creatures went to bed because they were perished with the cold. I mean, the house was cold. We didn't have radiators. There was one pipe running through the rooms. A lot of the sisters didn't need nursing care. They were just elderly people that needed minding and were they spoiled? I don't think so. They had so little. So maybe they were looking for a little bit of petting but there were very few comforts for them.

Then in 1974 I was elected superior. My mother was telling everybody. She was so proud, oh God. She was delighted. I can't say that I was as proud. I was superior and I was still teaching and we had a big community. I was going into that with utterly no training whatsoever, good, bad or indifferent. You brought your own integrity, which to me is very important, and you brought whatever skills you had, but the flip side of that was you brought your own baggage too. You had your strengths and your community's strengths, and you had your own weaknesses and the community's weaknesses. So it was a very mixed bag.

Flogging scripture study

The old structures were gone when I took over in 1974, and the new structures were coming in following Vatican II (1962–65). We had the new constitutions and statutes for our own diocese. We had drawn up our vision, our goal and our aims. The old order was gone. There was nothing in its place and we were trying to bring in a new order. A facilitator, Father James, was training us on how to hold meetings and how to talk one at a time. He said to me in his very grand accent, 'Now Sister, you will have no trouble with anything the sisters like. They will be delighted with the new freedoms, but when you try anything else you can expect it won't be as pleasant.' How right he was. It was great to be allowed to do things like going out to the hairdresser's, or to buy clothes, but when it came to things like study of scripture and renewing our lives, that was at another level. I think I was still very idealistic. People had no idea; they couldn't understand why I was flogging something like scripture study or these kinds of things.

The old order collapsed

Now I never cease to look back in amazement at how quickly the old order collapsed. I think, was it like a hollow shell and just one tap and it all went? The speed at which we lost all of the pious practices and everything else! Now in themselves all those things were very good, remembering the presence of God and when you met someone in the corridor greeting their angel guardian. The thinking behind that was about trying to be recollected and trying to work from the inside out, to bring that attitude to your work. I often felt, in my younger days too, that those things were being done as rituals rather than being meaningful. They had the potential to be meaningful but they had lost it. I think that is why when all the changes came all that stuff went. I'll tell you, we let go of them faster than we let go of the long skirts. And when you compare the struggle we had with the habit, my God, you wouldn't believe it.

To talk and do things

Vatican II was only giving the freedoms that were a normal part of everyday living. Permission to go out and buy your clothes was such a big thing for everybody. The change, to talk and to do things, to get that gate opened after four was huge. To be able to go down to the town and buy your own stamps was massive. To be able to get your skirt cleaned, to be able to buy something new, to be able to buy a pair of shoes were huge things. I mean, women are women are women! All that area of your life had been gone. I'd say in one sense they were great years, there was a kind of activity and excitement in the air.

Changing habits and people started dyeing the hair. Oh mother of God, will I ever forget it? The day of the change I saw the old ones coming down with grey heads and black heads and medium grey heads. Oh, I nearly fainted laughing! I was standing at the bottom of the stairs and I was dying laughing. It must have been awful hard on them. I was amazed at the ones who had actually dyed their hair, people who were quite conservative and here they come with the dyed hair! Ah sure, when you think of cutting the hair, it was cut at reception, literally, the whole bloody lot went! You were told that the hair was a woman's crowning glory. You were giving it all to Jesus, poor Jesus. When I think of it now I cringe. I didn't like it then but I like it less now. It wasn't good.

Everything ran smoothly

I'd say we did our best to change but I'm not sure, to this day, that anything has replaced what we had.

We had a structure in what I call the older, pre-Vatican II times. The advantage for the group was that everything ran quite smoothly. There was one person in charge. You knew what you were doing, you knew where you were going. There was a tremendous sense of support. Everybody was doing something the same, and there was a huge sense of security in that. There was a superior, there was a bursar, there was a mother assistant and there was a novice mistress. Each of them had her job. Then you had the senior stratum, your senior sisters and they had to be respected, or kowtowed to, depending on which word you want to use. I would make a distinction between both words and then there was the ordinary, the rank and file, you know, the chiefs and the Indians really. There was a great security and a place for everyone and everyone in their place. But it must have been only a shell because as soon as Vatican II came the whole deck of cards caved in. Without any warning that structure went away, and you were still trying to do your best but there weren't very many supports.

The superior no longer had the final say

I suppose the first thing that changed was obedience. Theoretically, the superior always had the final say but in practice everyone had her say. In the past the superior made the decisions and she told you, and it was lovely and you didn't contradict her. Now people began standing up for themselves or saying they were not doing this or that. The individual had a say, and a lot of the 'says' were not mature enough. One of our nuns had a great expression, 'meaning well but doing badly'. People weren't used to making a rational decision. There was also more group decision making, and you see that was a minefield because if you went with the majority rule it could be a very good decision or it could be a very bad decision.

Everybody was beginning to go their own way and stronger personalities began to emerge, people who would formerly have been under a good superior's thumb. They began to assert themselves and that made life difficult for others. God, how often we'd say, everyone is a reverend mother now, we've loads and loads of chiefs and very few Indians left, and that pertains to this day. Everybody wants independence. While I can see that each person is entitled to independence, I think that the good of the whole is greater than the good of one person, and I don't think the whole can be sacrificed for the good of one person. A lot of people wouldn't agree with me on that at all. They say, 'I'm entitled to this and I'm entitled to that, this is my right and I'm an individual'. I'll accept all that, but I still feel we committed ourselves to work as a group with a common vision. I still ask where is the mission now? Where is the focus now on our mission in the Church?

Many nuns gave up teaching and went into massaging people and the counselling thing too. I met a psychologist who said to me: 'Do you know one thing that is awful strange? The number of nuns that are studying counselling and they come up to us looking for jobs and I'll tell you the truth, I wouldn't put some of them in charge of a henhouse.' That's an outsider's view. A lot of the people who were doing this hadn't sorted themselves out at all. I wonder if it was a search for the unfulfilled. When you took out the spirit that motivated the early sisters to work for the poor then we became established, and it all became automatic and that spirit seemed to go and you worked on autopilot. Now I think there are a lot of unfilled lives. There was status then but there's not now. Religious life is not different to life in the world where self has become much more important than community. Religious house is only a microcosm of what is outside.

I don't think it was possible to renew

The work ethic was so strong and we were so committed to work that I don't think that it was possible for us to renew ourselves. You know, we had our Mass, we had our prayer, we had our meditation, we had our work in the school, we had our work in the hospital, we had our work in the community centre, we had our work on visitation and everybody was doing it. Then there was the call to go back to our source, to go back to the Gospel, to go back to our founding ideals. You would be saying to yourself, what is it that we are not doing? I think we were looking at it in terms of what more work we could be doing. I think that. I look back and say you would have needed to leave every apostolate if you were to put yourself into this new mode of thinking and living and renewal and back to the founder's vision. It was very hard and I know the Church called on us to do it.

So for the four years I did my level best. Without a doubt I worked very, very hard. I was whacked out. After two years I left teaching because there was so much to be done. It was a very difficult time, physically, emotionally and psychologically, every way. I felt as a human being I needed so much more than I had. I really did, and while every nun wanted to do as she wished when anything went wrong the buck rested with the superior. The older ones felt the younger ones could do what they liked. In actual fact the older ones also did what they liked. But this is how they saw it and to this day you'll still hear it. When I finished that I was very relieved. I really was very happy when it was over. As I say, I have no great qualms about it because I know I did my best, but it would be a poor best, looking at it now, in the sense that a bit more of training would have given me more skills. Anyway, it wasn't to be and maybe the Lord made up for that.

I was diagnosed with a heart problem

Life continued on after that. I went back to school and I did my work and my mother was still alive and I was looking after her and all that. So after she died I went out to the USA for a year. I couldn't cope with the heat at all. Oh my God, the heat, the heat, the heat! We didn't have any air conditioning. Ah, it was terrible! While I was out there I was diagnosed with a heart problem. So between the two things I said, 'Back home again now'. That's when I was appointed to a new convent.

There were about twelve there at the time. It was a great old place. The people were very friendly; the students were very, very nice. I was quite happy there but I did go through a period of very poor health then. I had a hysterectomy back in 1989. Oh God, I went downhill after that for a good while. I'd say it was probably a backlog of everything that came after the surgery. I got over the surgery. That was hard. I came back to school again and I took up remedial teaching. I retired in 2001 and I moved as leader to a small house.

There were blessings in coming here

When I was asked to come it never dawned on me to ask any questions. Now I look back on it the provincial had said, 'to help make community'. When I came here I found there were loads of young ones around but none of them would come here. When they knocked the convent the older nuns were very upset, as you would expect, and they sent them to this house. They put the younger ones out in rented houses. The change was coming that the younger people weren't willing to live with older people. I was asked to come because nobody else would come.

I was amazed at how much the move here took out of me. I came very willingly. The five years here gave me a huge emotional freedom and there was a huge healing in that. I was still doing my very best but I wasn't putting a pressure on myself to do it. I think that in the past I expected too much of myself. It has been a time for reflection and it's almost as if my whole life has come together.

My brother died very suddenly after heart surgery. I was just a year here when that happened. And that was particularly tough because I had to mourn on my own. My father and mother died and I grieved for them but it was nothing compared to the death of a sibling. My eldest sister died as well, but I suppose I had spent more time with my brother. The two of us were in the same kind of profession. There was that bond between us. That was hard and it was hard to mourn him here.

Here one of the nuns won't stay in this house alone. If I go for a walk she's inside the door waiting. Maybe it's fear, I don't know. And yet, when I say, 'Don't open the door', do you think she'll heed? Will she hell! Out she goes and it could be anyone who will give her a clout and knock her over. I see them in the big convent and when the superior goes out, they say, 'Where is she, we never see her'. She's there all day but just because they don't see her in their direct line of vision they worry. I think the mother figure being present makes them secure.

You were better to have humility

I could truthfully say that I always found religious life very hard. I'd look back and say yes, I found it hard. I don't think I got any favours in religious life in that I was never somebody's darling or never in the right place at the right time to get all the plaudits. In our early days there was this idea that if you had any bit of talent at all, you got nowhere with it. You were better to have humility. If you had talent there was a danger that you would get proud, so that talent wasn't used.

No developing of a sense of responsibility

I think I had a lot more potential than was ever developed. I didn't have the confidence, and religious life did not develop that confidence in me. It was hard to develop as a person. Your own personality didn't develop really. There was an effort at conformity. There was no developing a sense of responsibility because you weren't allowed to be responsible for anything. You had to do what everybody else was doing so I think the richness of people's personalities was missing. I mean, recreation was at four o'clock and everybody had to turn up with their sock to be darned. A companion of mine used to come with the socks and a needle and no thread in it and she spent the hour putting the needle in and out and we'd look over and be dying laughing. The whole bunch went out for a walk around the house at recreation time. In my early days we weren't let outside the gates at all. It was locked at four o'clock. I remember once as a postulant I was out walking and I was so fed up I started kicking stones. I pelted the stones down the drive in front of me. Oh gee! I got killed! I was told about religious decorum.

I'd say I suppressed my anger

When I entered there were some older nuns who would spend an awful lot of time in the chapel and they were very good, they were really genuine. Others spent an awful lot of time in the chapel and they could knock the head off you outside the chapel and that wouldn't be into my book at all. I reckon people took out their anger on the next one. You might say something to somebody and they'd cut the nose off you and you'd say, 'Oh what did I say or what did I do?' Maybe something else had happened and you were the nearest one. I always think about the yarn about the man who was up all morning because he was going on the train. He was up at all hours and he was ready. God almighty, whatever happened to him didn't he arrive at the station and the blessed train was just pulling out. The poor old porter had bent down to pick up something and the man gave him a running kick, 'You and your oul train', he said. I think that happens in life all the time. I think it does.

I'd say I suppressed my anger. It came out in illness. Mother of God, sure we kept the private hospitals going for years. Yes we did. It came out in illness definitely. Ah, it did. Sure there were creatures that used go up to the hospital for a holiday. The consultants made a fortune on us. You don't see that happening nowadays. There was an awful lot of illness. People ill and getting tonics and going over to the doctor every day and I think all these things were cries for help. I'd say they were looking for comfort.

You would pay the price if you spoke your mind. Oh you'd be cut down to size. You might talk about things among your friends but by God you wouldn't say it to superiors. When I think of the orphanages and people say, 'Oh, where were the other nuns?' But if you were a junior sister and someone was senior to you there was no way you could go to a superior and complain because you wouldn't be listened to. When people say they can't understand where the others were I can understand where they were. I think you wouldn't be listened to and I think you would be ostracised. The people in charge would let you know they didn't like it. The people who were in charge, they were like God. They might not have been the first person of the Blessed Trinity but they were probably the second. They were just God Almighty; you daren't even suggest that some of them might be wrong.

The blind eye

In the past I think that superiors knew things but they covered everything, the blind eye. I think some were afraid of the strong personalities who were stronger than superiors. Today nobody wants to be a superior. Nobody is able to take the amount of hassle and what people expect from somebody in charge. They are just not able for it and nobody will do it in today's world. It is because of the difficult people. They're for sale; they're for sale! I

think we are talking about people with either personality disorder or people whose personality did not suit religious life. They
shouldn't have been kept, but superiors weren't strong enough
or weren't able or hadn't the courage to send them home. Everybody in the community would have recognised this. I entered in
1955 and no one was ever sent away. One or two left all right.

There were people who knew how to play the system. I was
never able to do that because if I didn't like something you'd see
it in my face immediately. I mean, you could see the new superior being elected and she would have a cohort immediately of
friends and when she'd go out of office that cohort could move
on to the next one. I couldn't do that. I just couldn't do it. I wasn't
able for that at all. Maybe I was too straight for my own good.

Self was becoming important

Today in chapters there is a rarefied atmosphere. You just
wouldn't believe what people come up with. There is a team in
charge. Once I said to a member of a team, 'You know such and
such a thing is daft', and she said, 'You know these things are
drawn up and we have to implement them because that is the
charge we are given, to implement the decisions of the chapter'.
But you can get awful queer stuff. I can tell you that even still you
can get a handful of very strong people in a chapter. They might
start a project and get tired of it after a very short time, and they
beautifully hand it over to somebody else who is left literally carrying the baby. I think there are people who are not able to be see
a thing through, see it through to the bitter end.

I know houses where there might be three and they never
meet, they never sit down to a meal together. They mightn't even
talk to each other. They might not be fighting with each other,
but they say, 'It's my life'. Now this thing has crept in, 'my life'
and sense of self and I have to have this, and I have to have that,
and I have to have the other. This is where single living has come

in. There was never a decision at congregational level to go into single living and yet it's all over the place. Somebody decided and got permission to do it and it took off. You have everybody going her own way and the sky is the limit. I don't know what we are about now. If I were to go to a chapter and say what I have just said to you I'd be bombed out of it. I'd literally be bombed out of it! You are a marked person when you speak your truth that way. Some people can be very strong when they get back at you, even if they perceive that you are saying something about them, so I don't know where that can bring us.

First it started with going into smaller houses but people found out that it was difficult. Those who are living on their own are finding that I have to look after myself, I have to cook for myself, I have to clean, I have to shop, I have to do everything and some of them are finding that quite difficult and they're wondering could that be improved on. So there's an air of unreality about life. Now there's a move back again to bigger units.

The disintegration of the congregation

With the individual's gain in personal freedom the organisation suffered. I mean, you had people beginning to be free to say things, to think things, to do things. Then who is the person at the top who is able to hold that together and keep the aims and the ideals of the congregation? So really Vatican II brought about the disintegration of the congregation in a way. It had been going on autopilot for years. I think it would have disintegrated even if Vatican II had never happened. A lot of those structures would have fallen. They had to. You can only keep things like that going for so long but I think that Vatican II hastened them.

That's where I will pitch my tent

I'll be nearly seventy-three when this house closes. At that hour of my life to start living on my own in an apartment is not for me.

A small house, small houses, are grand if you have people who are compatible but you are very much in each other's faces and I think it is more difficult. Most of the nuns that I am friendly with are in my original convent. They are the people that I was young with and I said that's where I'll pitch my tent. It is a big convent, a huge convent. Down the years that will go. There must be about forty-nine bedrooms and only sixteen people in it. Now a good friend of mine put it to me very well when she said, 'I never realised how old the old were until the young left'.

Where is my support now?

I think it's downhill from now on. I think it's endgame, historically too, most active apostolic congregations lasted about two hundred years. The amount of change that has happened in my religious life is enormous. The earth went totally from under us. I know what my life is about, but what are we about as a province at the moment? I'm not sure that this going into a big unit with apartments and separate houses will do us any good at all. If we go back to the pre-Vatican II times and see the support then the question is, where is my support now? You do the best you can but there is nobody to catch you if you are falling. There is sadness. The pendulum has swung and ideally you'd like to bring it back to the middle again. I often find myself thinking, I would love to be able to leave all this and start off something totally new or different.

We're paddling and we're drowning

There was a whole sea change really and the outside world changed radically as well. I think that the older structures saved us. To a degree there was more solidarity. Now there are no structures outside and there are no structures inside. We are like the two frogs on top of the bucket of milk. Do you know that story? Two frogs fell into a bucket of milk and one fellow gave up the fight after a while, and the other fellow kept paddling and he actually made butter and he landed on top of the butter. We're all like the two frogs now, we're paddling and we're drowning and we're coming up for air and we're doing the best we can but it's difficult. For the people in charge now it's more management of a dying structure than leading a vibrant group, and yet sometimes when you get a group together at a big meeting you say there is great life yet. My final words: 'If there is no God I'll be rightly stuck.'

9

Lily

'Were there things happening and I didn't see them?'

Introduction

Lily is fifty-six years of age. She left her office job and moved to Ireland to become a nun because she wanted to work with children and she liked the contemplative aspect of the active order she joined. Her family had emigrated to England but returned to Ireland soon after she entered.

Lily left school with little self-belief because a teacher told her she would never do any good. As she now awaits her MA conferring she can leave her feelings of inferiority behind. At present she is contending with a terminal illness.

Novitiate life was puzzling for Lily. She was so busy she didn't have time to think and everything had to be done a certain way and permission had to be sought for even the least significant thing. Being creative or showing initiative was not part of the culture. Lily felt astonished and depersonalised when she had to mark her clothes with a number. In general, she felt bewildered and uncomfortable and decided if this continued she would not stay. One morning those bad feelings were replaced by what she described as 'no feeling'. This seemed to be the only way to survive in this institution and she succumbed to this conditioning. She was in the process of losing her individuality in favour of a collective identity. She was beginning to become institutionalised.

As a postulant Lily had a placement with blind children and she thought she would like to do this work, but the practice of not giving nuns the work they liked still continued in this convent. Her placements in two of the Magdalen homes run by her order were a nightmare. She was afraid of the women; they may have projected their fear onto her. Once again she found she couldn't think. She made a joke of doing the sums as a diversion from the pain of working with these women. It was the regimentation of the laundry that upset her, something also felt by the nuns in the closed system of the convent. She felt the provincial who lived in the convent was watching her. The women in the laundry were under constant surveillance.

When Lily saw the film The Magdalene Sisters *she worried that it highlighted similar conditions to those in which she had worked. She is aware of the institutionalisation of the women in the laundry and of the nuns with whom she is living at this time. Institutionalisation is an internalisation of a culture. Nobody questioned. She wonders about the Magdalens' lack of a chance of making a relationship with the opposite sex, which she says the nuns had. This is not the experience of the older sisters. What Lily forgets is that many Magdalens had already had a sexual experience, and it was for that reason that they were committed to the institution. They had deviated from the rigid expectations of the Church that were imposed on society in Ireland at the time. All liability was inflicted on the women. The men were not locked away for their part in the sexual acts that led the Magdalens to be taken out of society, and often led to the children of these unions being put into industrial schools. Neither society nor the Church see men as culpable or answerable when it comes to sexual trans-gression.*

Although Lily's first real work assignment with children at twenty-three years of age was in the dreaded St. Mary's, she was anxious to get started. The house was in a dreadful state and she soon turned it around by being kind but strict. After a few years she was sent to train for one year. As time went on conditions for the sisters changed and they began to work with lay staff and get time off. Eventually, the whole regime changed and there were meetings and reviews for the children. The nuns had to decide whether or not to continue in the work. Lily decided she was ready to move on. An inspector from the Health Board questioned her about a man who was subsequently convicted and jailed for abuse in one of the houses. She believes that it was because of the constant activity that one did not have the time to know what was happening in another house. However, she has some concept of the unconscious process of turning a blind eye and she worries about that.

When the convent closed Lily's group joined another community and life became more difficult because the two groups were so different. Lily felt she was in a time warp. She had no privacy and when a new convent with a lot of glass was built that was the last straw. Personal exposure was the new form of institution-alisation. She had a sense of panic about her inability to come to terms with the state of affairs, and she found it impossible to maintain her equilibrium. She regressed and began to act in a childish manner, mirroring the way she felt she was being treated by the authorities who deprived her of her voice. The authorities annoyed her, so she deliberately annoyed the old-fashioned nuns.

Lily feels that the older nuns have not been able to adapt to the changes that have come about. Their continued emphasis on mindless activities is likely to have been a desperate attempt to assure themselves that things have not changed. These nuns resist change, not through stubbornness, but from an actual inability to change their way of life because they have been cut off from the real world for so long.

The superficial was good enough for the provincial when she came for visitation. She had no desire to look beyond the obvious. She was unable or unwilling to pick up on the fear of speaking out, and was either unable or chose not to address Lily's inability to conform. In retrospect, it is easy to be critical of the provincial, but it is likely that she had no training for her role. The collaboration between the authorities and the nuns, advocated by Vatican II, did not seem to be working successfully when the superiors did not listen to the nuns in relation to building a new convent and resulted, ultimately, in Lily deciding to leave the convent.

Having left, Lily had many adjustments to make, not least finding her individual identity through her choice of dress. She is not yet confident about that. Loneliness and loss were part of her grieving process and breaking with the culture of putting oneself last was a difficult habit to break.

She makes an important point on religious life when she says that the institution does not question itself. It is always assumed that it is the individual that is at fault when people leave, and earlier in her life Lily blamed herself instead of the institution when she could not cope. When she worked in the Magdalen laundry she said nobody questioned, they just got on with it. In this institution the status quo was accepted. She also thinks that many nuns would not have the courage to leave although they might wish to do so. Her journey has changed although her work has continued and will continue as long as she is able.

In the novitiate Lily succumbed to institutionalisation to accomplish her agenda of working with children. Her success in working with deprived children and her broadening of her hori-

zons through further education helped her to see a bigger picture. This made her return to the regular convent and small-mindedness of older nuns who resisted change, in an effort to believe it hadn't happened, intolerable. She used humour as a defence and eventually realised the futility and insincerity of this defence and she returned to the world. There is a sense that she could not reveal all she knew about residential childcare.

Lily's Story:

The teacher told me I'd never do any good

I started school in England. I was about five when I got there. I found photographs since, they're of me when I was about four and I was living in Ireland so I'd say I was brought to Manchester in time for school. And every school holidays we came back to Ireland, back to my grandmother's house. I didn't go to university after leaving school. I went to work because my family couldn't afford to send anyone to university. It wasn't the thing. I would love to have done art or something. But I think of the great sense of achievement I have in getting my MA. I am so excited about that. Excited, number one, because of the circumstances under which I did it, you know, my illness. It's the only thing I ever wanted to achieve all my life because a teacher once told me I'd never do any good. That has never left me until now. I have told everyone to watch me when I go for my MA conferring. I'm going to have high shoes, with noise. I'm putting bells on them because I want everyone to hear me as well as see me. And it's such a wonderful thing for me to achieve this.

At the moment things are not going so well at the hospital. They're telling me things aren't too great. I wasn't going to tell you, but I will because it's very prominent in my head at the moment. I suppose it's the thing that's making me tick. I got cancer six years ago and it came back last year. They said to me the other day that it's gone to other places and that they are a bit concerned. They want to give me a few more tests and they're talking about pain relief. So that doesn't sound too good.

I suppose it's making me think about the value of life. It's making me think about where I'm going and what I plan to do. It's there and we have to carry on. I said to myself, 'You're not going to get any more chemo and you're not going to be getting off work on Thursday'. I feel a great sense of peace. Now this may change and I may become very angry. I'm going to make the most of this. It makes me think of living every day as if I hadn't another one. It's an absolutely great feeling. I wonder does that come back to the training as a religious.

One morning I got up and there was no feeling

After school I worked at a good job in an office in Manchester where my mother wanted me to be and I hated it. Then I moved down to London and my headmistress from school was able to get me a job working with children. Prior to entering the convent, I had this holy sense that I was going to be different. I was young and I didn't know what I was letting myself in for. What really drew me was some spiritual sense. There was a draw. I went to every dance. I went to every picture. I went to everything that was on. I thought this draw might go away. Why do I want to do this? Wouldn't it be great if I could just do like everybody else? It would make life very easy for me. There was a call, without a doubt, a draw to do something with my life, more than I was doing. It was the contemplative-active aspect of religious life that I liked, so that's what drew me. I have no regrets for doing it because a lot of what I did and learned I brought with me and I'm still using. I entered the convent in 1972 and my family had moved over to Ireland by the time I was in community.

On the second day in the convent I couldn't cope with the black and white. I had to see colours. So I said to the Novice Mistress, 'I can't cope with this, I'm getting a pain in me head looking at black and white', and she sent me over to the school where there were special needs children. I came back, 'I'm all right now, it's just I couldn't cope with no colours'. I like colour. So anyway, that was good. My Novice Mistress was excellent and she is still very much alive and when things happen to me she turns up. She was a very human, sincere woman and we got on very well. She always looked for the good in everyone.

Looking back, maybe I didn't understand what I was doing. It is interesting that the whole day was filled, you didn't have time to think. Maybe it was easier not to think. The day went on with morning prayer, Mass, breakfast and then there was some manual work. I didn't like that. It had to be done in a certain way. Why it had to be done in a certain way I really didn't know, and maybe I still don't know. Special prayer at ten o clock and then you went off and you did more prayers and reading and that brought you to lunch. After lunch you had a break. There was music and I remember them saying, 'Please sister, can I have music?' And I was wondering why they were asking. Why could she not just put it on and be done with it!

When I entered they were putting numbers on clothes. My number was 253 and I thought, imagine, I am only a number! Well, if I feel like this after a few weeks I'm not staying here. I can't be bothered with this. If I have this bad feeling, or this uncomfortable feeling I'll know it's not for me. Well, anyway, one morning I got up and there was no feeling and I thought, oh, this is alright. Everybody seemed to know what they were doing except me. Three of us entered together and we were the first to keep our own names and it was a very nice group of people. I think that I really enjoyed the novitiate. I enjoyed the fun of it because there were a lot of young people and I had great fun. On my second or third week somebody left the convent. We didn't know where she went and when I said, 'Where is Sister Mary?' nobody answered me. They all looked at one another and I thought there must be something wrong. There was that bewilderment about things.

This is terrible to do this to these people

As a postultant they sent you on 'an outing'. Some outing! The idea was that you went into community to see what it was like to live there. I was sent to the Magdalen laundry. Never to be forgotten. I was there about two months and, oh God, I'll never forget it. I hated it. I absolutely hated it. I hated it, hated every minute of it. I suppose I was young and I was afraid of the women. They were all into this laundry business and I wasn't a bit interested in it. I had to be totting up and every so often I would shout, 'four nines, what are four nines?' I couldn't add it up quickly enough! I couldn't even think because I didn't like it.

But the sisters were very kind. You see, I wasn't the same as them because I wasn't professed. So I had to keep doing my own stuff like going to bed at a certain time, getting permission for certain things and all that. The worst of it was that the provincial lived in the house so I really was on the spot. I felt I was being watched. I was working with the Magdalens and getting the experience of having a job, being able to plan, pray and work and mingle everything together, as you would as a professed sister.

Next we had a spiritual year and we didn't go anywhere. I didn't know how I was going to cope with this. That was fine and then the second year of your novitiate you were sent out again. This time I was sent to work with the blind. And I worked with the staff and the children. I got an idea of what disability was about for them and their families and I really enjoyed that. It was great. I thought, this is good, I like it and then the Novice Mistress said, 'you won't be doing that'. So that was a good start!

This was a nightmare again, they sent me to another laundry. They were determined to put me in a laundry, and I was determined I wasn't going! So I was there for two months and then I was back. It was a nightmare. I think it was the whole regimentation of it. This was all the women seemed to know. Some of them were there because they had babies and what was wrong with that? I was a bit ahead of my time and I thought this was awful. A lot of the women were elderly and they had lived their lives like this. I found it very difficult and I was living with older sisters as well. I wasn't used to that because in the novitiate I had loads of young people.

I think the superiors were really testing me and I didn't like it. I told them that too. And they asked why and I said because I didn't like this work. I didn't like it. I don't like doing sums. I don't like counting sheets and how much they cost and wasn't there more to life than this, anybody could do this. You didn't need a sister to do this but at the same time we were there for a reason, to give time to those people. We used to give a lot of time to them. They needed a lot of one to one. But I felt drained by them because we couldn't give enough. That's how I found it difficult and the minute I got with the children I knew I was okay.

There were no babies. The babies were adopted. It was nearly like that film *The Magdalene Sisters*. When I went to see it, it really had an awful effect on me. I thought maybe I was in the middle of that. Some of the women told me they were locked in their rooms years ago and I think the whole thing of the institutionalisation affected me. So I found that very difficult. I was still in the noviceship where it was very much rules and regulations. When I was with young people we could see the funny side of things, whereas now I was in a more professional position. I was a sister now, even though I was a novice, they saw me as a sister, and that was quite shocking for me because I didn't see myself as that yet.

Some of the women were in their forties, and the rest in their twenties and what had they done? Now, they seemed to be happy enough. Some of them left and went into sheltered housing. Some of them went outside working. A lot of them didn't want to leave. This was fascinating because some of them were quite able and capable of holding jobs outside. But they were so involved with inside they didn't want to leave. This was their home. I suppose some of them had mental health problems, which may not have been identified the way we would be able to identify them now. They grated on others and they used to fight. In one of the homes I had to do meal duty. This was nearly the finish of me, to sit while they had their meals. I don't know why, you just sat there on a kind of a podium and I thought this was terrible. I felt I was trying to control these women. And they were all right, they didn't need me to control anything. I don't even know why I was there but I had to do it, and I thought, this is terrible to do this to these people.

Some of the Magdalens would have had babies but not all; there were criminal offences and no support from family. One of them told me she stole a bicycle and she was brought to the Garda station and the whole thing took off from there. She was in her sixties. The lack of a chance of making a relationship with the opposite sex was a thing that struck me because they were all women. How did they deal with their sexuality, and while community is similar you had exposure to the opposite sex. Well, I did because I always had a male figure with the children. We had a fellow who came in to play soccer and we had clerical students and we had an American priest who did his tertianship. So I did have a bit more exposure to men than those women who had nothing.

The sisters in both houses were lovely to me. Of course, they were institutionalised as well. Nobody questioned, they just got on with it. And I was thinking, I can't do this. I can't do this. If this is it I don't want it. The Novice Mistress said to me, 'How are you getting on?'

'I hate it, I hate it, and I want out of it, as quick as lightning.'

'You can't come out of it as quick as lightning but we know now you don't want that.'

They were really trying to find a field for me, to know where to put me. Although I had worked with children prior to that they just wanted to be sure.

When I was professed there was still a mystery about everything. The profession day was a great day and a lovely day for family and it was a great achievement as I saw it. I had no doubts about what I was doing. I knew why I was going to do this. I was quite happy even though there was bits of it I didn't like, but then there's bits of life I didn't like as well, so I was okay.

This house was called a madhouse

I said I wanted to do childcare and I got what I wanted. I was sent to St Mary's and I had a dread of St Mary's, an absolute dread. I had heard novices had gone there and every one of them had got hepatitis. There were kids running loose and there were places being set on fire and people were blaming the children in care. And I thought that must be an awful place. I couldn't believe my ears when she said, 'You're going to St Mary's'. I was about twenty-three. I was full of enthusiasm. Couldn't get to it quick enough.

I arrived on a Friday, first of October, at 8.00 p.m., never to be forgotten. I had my tea in the convent and I went straight over to this big institution. It was split into different units. There were houses like group homes but I had no concept of that. A lay person, Joan, opened the back door to let me in and the first thing she said was, 'You don't know how welcome you are!' I thought, I wonder is that good? I knew that I was in this big place and I wondered how I was going to find my way in and out of it and survive.

I'm going to make a go of this was my gut feeling the minute I arrived. I was delighted I got the job I wanted. Even though it was St Mary's and the fact that worried me most about St Mary's was that they cooked their own food in the houses. I thought, I can't cook, how am I going to cope with this? In fact, when I arrived and saw what was in front of me I completely forgot about cooking. A lady was cooking and I didn't think she was very good. So I put the run on her. When she saw me tasting the food before I gave it to the children it didn't go down too well. I used to do things like that because if I couldn't eat it they shouldn't have to.

The first night Joan gave me keys and there were hundreds of them I thought. She said, 'There's a bunch of keys, that one is your room'.

'But I won't need the others because I'm only going to bed.'

'You will.'

I went to bed. I had no idea how many children were outside my door. Really, I was very gullible. I was afraid to look at them in case they'd wake up or they'd ask me anything and I wouldn't know what to do. When I woke I heard the sound of a mouth organ and I thought, how am I going to walk out there and pass these? I went out and they were gone and a bell rang and I went to Mass. I saw the two altar boys who were serving Mass and I thought, I wonder if I have to mind them? See, I only thought of minding. I hadn't the concept of all that went with this childcare. I discovered that a whole family had been admitted the first night while I slept and I never heard them. They were beside themselves with distress. I'll never forget it. I didn't know what to do with them.

There was nothing in the house. The children had broken everything. The sitting room consisted of a piano, a record holder with no records, an old table and chairs that had been broken and jumped on and a television. I thought, this is terrible! A dirty carpet, this is awful! How can children do any good here if it's like this? Up to eighteen sisters had passed through that particular house, between novices and people doing placements, and they didn't stay because this house was called a madhouse, it was so chaotic. There was butter on the walls and the children used to throw things. They used to break furniture and everything. One night, when I was in bed, they were all getting up to break the furniture and I gave them all a hurley and I said, 'Break all you want and then when we have it all broken we won't have anything and we won't have to worry.' I think I said it because there was nothing much in the sitting room. There was a piano and a table.

I thought animals would be good

After some time the provincial was coming and there was a big hooha! She was coming for visitation and they said to me, 'You must make something of this house'. We put up curtains and we started clearing presses and we got rid of the rubbish. The manager let me shop so eventually we got stuff. I got new couches and I said if we are going to make anything of this we've got to get the equipment to do it.

I got a goldfish and a turtle. Dogs and cats were out of the question. I thought animals would be good to get the children to respect them. So I had that kind of insight. I remember there was one child in the group who had a speech impediment and couldn't speak. His was the first birthday party we ever had. We did it with a packet of balloons, a box of bubbles and a cake from the shop and it was the best party ever because it had never been done before. One lad was very talented and his job was to play the piano for us all in the morning, beautiful. Everyone else had to sweep and clean and his job was to play. There was a lad who said he could still remember the day he met me. I had a pound of butter and a tin of beans in my hands. I taught him to play marbles and I gave him tea on a tray, brought tea and biscuits into the sitting room. We sat down and we watched television just to be together, to get a sense of being able to sit without having a row. I just settled into it and I was there for eighteen years.

Things started to get better

I was off for the whole year 1979/80 while I was training in childcare. It was great. They got somebody in to do my job. It gave me a sense of community living as well. I was a great woman on a bike and I was on it day and night. That was my salvation. I used to go to town every day to see what was going on. I learned to drive and that gave me great scope, a great sense of freedom. If anyone in the community wanted to go to Dublin or to be dropped to meetings I was very ready and well able. I learned all the roads in Dublin from that.

I never had a room in the convent because there was no room. So I lived in the institution and I went over to the convent for breakfast, dinner and tea, plus prayers and sitting down in the afternoon. I made great friends there. The sisters were lovely and the majority of them were young. There was a great spirit in that community. If you went home for a few days, the table was set in the kitchen when you came back and they would all come to see how you got on.

We always slept with the children at that time. Then times advanced and the lay staff slept with them and they gave us a night off. So they gave us a room in the convent. Things started to get better and we got a day off in the week which was great. I always remember the first night I went to the pictures. It would have been a big thing going out but I was advanced then. I had got training and I had met other people and I began to mix with the other side of the community, and there were events to do with the course coming up and I had to attend them. Some of the older sisters had never done that and they used to wonder.

I used to want to kill her sometimes

I got on very well with the manager. She had been thirty years there and she had worked her way up to manager. She was the one who had everything in her head. She was a walking encyclopaedia! There were no social workers or anything like that. She was in charge of the whole centre, six houses, and a nun in charge in each house. She was a good manager. There were no meetings then and there were no such thing as reviews for the children. We didn't have a clue.

The manager was worried when the task force came out. You couldn't have more than eight children in a house. We had been dealing with fourteen at a time. There were seventeen at the time I came. I used to say, 'I saw him this morning, but I didn't see him since'. But you see all that bureaucracy frightened us. It frightened us who had such leeway. We'd hear, 'the Health Board said and the Health Board said'. I said, 'The Health Board must talk about nothing except St. Mary's. They mustn't have a thing to do except talk about us.' I was that sick of listening to it but in actual fact they weren't saying it half the time but she was so keyed up.

We moved by night

Eventually they moved all the children. We were in St Mary's up until they decided they were going to close it. This was a big thing. Our new group home was up the road, so we moved them all up there, physically moved them ourselves. We moved by night. I had a great friend, a sister, and we moved with two prams. We put wardrobes on top of prams and we used to keep our heads behind the wardrobes so people wouldn't see who was walking. We did it when the children were in bed.

It was a great breakthrough for the children to live in the community. They could make friends and they were no different to others. Having them in the community, mixing and getting involved in the activities, going to the shops, getting jobs, that was a good thing. When they were in St Mary's the children wouldn't say where they lived, they wouldn't give the address. They wouldn't bring friends home or anything. Then they started bringing friends home. I always remember when one brought the boyfriend for afternoon tea. To see her reaction I said to her, 'Do you think I should wear my veil for this occasion?'

'Don't put a veil on you. Don't, and get rid of that nun that's screaming. Don't have her here when he comes!'

'Would you like me to introduce myself?'

'I'll introduce you!'

But the children were beginning to have a bit of life. They were beginning to live like everybody else.

It was like a family and I got as much out of it as they did. And we had our rows I'm telling you. But if they were blamed in the wrong as they often were I didn't allow it, 'it must be the children from the home, it has to be'. It wasn't because I had them here and I knew they were here because I saw them. They did things, stole stuff, they stole things out of my pocket and I used to say, 'I know it's gone and I know who took it but I'm not going to fall out with you'. Sometimes things came back. Sometimes they didn't. We had our rows and I'm sure some of them would say I wasn't fair and others would say I was, because they have said that in all these investigations. They have said, 'Yes, she was fair, she was tough'. The only way I pulled it together was doing good things with the children, doing things that they'd remember, and that might bring them round, with little but with great fun. I got great praise from the provincial as I pulled it together.

We were afraid to let go

When the social workers came in they started having internal reviews for each child. Then statutory reviews were introduced and each child had to have a social worker. That was the beginning. We didn't take children in in bulk any more. We tried to keep families together but it didn't always work out that way. The key worker system gave authority to the lay people, which we were afraid to let go of. That was a good thing. Now we got only four children and we had a budget system and cash.

The sisters had to reflect on what they were doing. Personally, I had to because if I was sitting in with a senior social worker and a social worker and the manager I really needed to be alert, to know the children. I did the course in Trinity in 1992 and I saw that one to one work with children was brilliant. The thirty-year manager left and a new manager came and she was very visible. She wanted to get the sisters in order in the sense of looking after themselves. That was the first thing she did. Were we looking well and did we dress well and all these things? We were going to conferences and meetings. The whole thing of attachment came up there and I'm still at it. When we were nineteen we didn't know whether the children were attached or not because we were too busy physically holding it together. The whole thing of training and of being exposed to conferences made each one either go with it or come out of it. I couldn't do residential any longer. I just didn't have it and maybe that was because I had other plans for my life.

Were there things happening and I didn't see them?

If you look back it was all activity. The Health Board interviewed me about the abuse in St Mary's. This fellow got a ten-year sentence for abusing boys. I didn't know him. Thank the Lord I was gone when he came. Then, in the summing up, the interviewer said, 'You hardly had time to know what was going on'. There were one hundred and nine children in that centre and there was one manager and there were six houses and there was a sister in each house and everybody was busy. I said, 'The houses were all very separate and we didn't know what was going on because we didn't have time to know what was going on'.

You don't know what anyone is going to say and you don't know the accuracy either. You meet a lot of people on your journey and you don't know. Yes, and a lot of them would have said to me, 'I got money'. I'd say, 'Good for you, if you got it and you need it okay', but I never got into it. I never asked why or how. But then again the children are so damaged and money is a great draw. The tabloids would say, 'Do you want money for your story?' Now I've met people who have been through the system and have been to the redress board. There's an element of anger to it.

There's no comeback for us if our name arises. We've no comeback. You just go with it because there isn't any redress board for the people who are called up. I'm sure people say about me, 'She was all right, but she was unfair to me on this occasion'. I wasn't always doing it right. When it comes up I wonder what did I do? Did I do it right? I have those thoughts you know. Would I do it the same again or were there things happening and I didn't see them?

We were gone back in time

I could no longer live religious life when St Mary's closed and the children moved. When the convent closed we went to live with another community. It was the same order but you'd think we were two different orders. They never went out anywhere while we were on the road every day mixing with the people. I felt that we were gone back in time. We were out in the country, and the older sisters had no way of coming into town. I was totally against the move and nobody would listen. We wanted a small house in town like many of the orders had but that did not happen. I'll never forget it, we were all huddled together and it was more institutionalised than where I'd come from. Oh, I couldn't cope with that. Everyone would know where you were, what you were doing, what time you did it, how you did it!

A very powerful lady

When a new superior was coming to the community we heard she was the best thing. It wasn't the case at all when she arrived. I felt that she could bring us down, because of her abuse of power, and her inaccurate memory. She was a very powerful lady who if she didn't get you on the spot, she'd get you later. There was an element of abuse in it, verbally and emotionally. She had a controlling way and yet you could meet her five minutes later and she would be lovely as if nothing had happened.

She was very kind to me when I was leaving. Maybe she was glad I was going. She watched what I ate and she had all the little things I liked in a box to start me off. She used to go for a walk with me in the evenings but I couldn't trust her. Fear stops people trusting.

There's something wrong with me

Then they built a new convent in this day and age and hardly anyone entering. I thought that was the daftest thing ever. And we had to all move in there then. That was a nightmare. It was a huge complex, a square, it was all glass so everywhere you moved, everyone saw you. I used to wander in one door and out the other, just to annoy them. If I didn't come in, they'd ask where did she go? Where is she? What is she doing? Is she coming in for tea? Maybe she won't come for tea. Oh, good Lord! I began to think there's something wrong with me. I'm not able to do this, so I thought I must leave, I must leave. I'm not going to stay here. I can't do this, because I felt I was insincere about the whole religious life.

She'd blow the thing up high

As I said the superior was a very forceful lady who liked to stand very near you and talk down to you. 'There's a smell in here,' she used to say and I'd pretend I never heard her. I used to tell her I was deaf. I used to say, 'I don't smell anything', and I'd been eating curried chips! I had gone for a counselling course in Trinity. And I didn't get it or I wasn't asked about it or I wasn't sent for. I thought that was very strange. I had told her I was going for that. And I never heard a word about it. I decided that I'd apply for the child protection and welfare in Trinity and I didn't tell anybody about it. I went for the interview and I never told anybody. So I went up to her and I said, 'You heard of the course I didn't get in Trinity.'

'I knew you wouldn't get Trinity.'

'Well, I got another course.'

'What is it?'

'It's child protection and welfare.'

'Where is it?'

'Trinity!'

Well, Lord God, if you saw the face of her, she was furious. Anyway, when things didn't agree with her she used to play the organ. We used to have evening prayer after tea. When things weren't good or if there was a tiff at all she'd blow the thing up high. She'd have the volume up on high doh. The minute I heard the music I thought we're bad, tonight. It's gone down very well! And they all knew. I had great fun.

I had great fun with those kinds of things but you can only do that for so long. You have to stop and ask what it's about, and I really wasn't being sincere.

I thought this is it

When the jobs came in for community childcare workers I thought this is it. Getting the job in the Health Board was a nightmare, a living nightmare. I had to go the provincial to ask permission to go for the job, to apply for it. So I wrote to her. But they said that they never did anything like that before. And I said, 'Well maybe it's the best way to do it'.

'But we usually pray about it.'

'I'm worn out praying, worn down praying about it.'

The social workers had told me about the job. They told me to go for it because I would be brilliant at it. I got the job and that was the praying I was doing and I was going to take it. The nuns nearly went mental. In other orders, the nuns were all out in jobs and here we were messing about like this. They nearly went out of their minds because it was never done. They thought it was desperate because normally you are missioned. I told my boss that. She's lovely. We still laugh about it. She said, 'I wonder now would they like to know in head office that you are missioned here to me!'

The day I started the job I had to go to the principal social worker to present myself. When I went to her she started to introduce me to everybody as Sister Lily and I said to her, you don't need to do that. You don't need to say sister, just tell them I'm Lily. I wanted to dissociate myself from it, even before I left, by saying, 'Don't call me sister'. I used to say it to the children when we went shopping. They were awful for shouting out in Dunnes Stores, roaring your name all over the place, and the reason I was saying it then was I was trying not to make them different. Little did I know how different we looked! Two big trolleys, what were we like? When you think about it, and we thought we were great because we had no habits. We were doing the best we could and all these trailing after us like the Pied Piper with the two trolleys. And we thought we were great!

I was just performing

I felt I couldn't live the religious life in the community because I wasn't sincere about it. I didn't want to come home from work. I wasn't happy coming home. I felt I'm not part of this so why am I doing it? I was just performing. I went into the chapel one evening, and I said, 'Please God will you send some sign to me that I am to stay here or go because I can't take much more of this. I can't be sincere and I can't be insincere. I can't do it. If you want to hold me you'd better do something quick. If you want to send me somewhere, if you want me to do something you'd better do something quick.' And when I went into my tea I heard there was going to be visitation. A visitation is when the superior general comes to visit the house. Oh, I thought, there's an answer to prayer. Did anyone ever get an answer so quick? I went in and I laughed the whole way through the tea because they were all wondering what would she be saying, what would she be doing, what would she be looking for, and I thought, I really don't care, but I'll be looking for her and wait until I get her.

Now within days there were new toilet roll holders and there was this and there was that and I thought that was all kind of show business and I don't like that. People see me as I am. I said, 'It's a pity she didn't come sooner, we'd be posher!' I used to say things like that. I think people were afraid.

It takes courage to speak out and some people may not have the courage. I certainly would not have had the courage to speak out to that extent. I was going to say, 'This is not for me'.

She asked me, 'How do you find the community?'

And I said, 'What community?' back to her because I don't feel part of this, and maybe it's my own doing but I just couldn't settle myself in it. She offered me anything that I wanted. Was there anything that they could do to help me? I had been two years thinking about it. And it took me about a year to come out from under it then.

I never told the community. I never told anybody. I just said I have to work this through myself and the first people I told was my family. And I made the call outside of the community, that'll show you how untrusting I was. The new superior general was appointed and I wrote to her. She sent for me promptly once she got the letter. I'd say that was the first letter she got. She was very nice and she asked, would I take a year? I said, 'Yes'. I'd be delighted to take a year and we'd look at it then.

My mother and father eloped

I had a cottage rented. Nobody knew, nobody knew that I had got a car. My brother-in-law got it for me. I had it all done. My mother and father eloped when they got married and I literally eloped the same way. I didn't keep contact with the sisters once I left. I felt I'm either going to leave or I'm not going to leave. I'm not going to be in and out, I'm going to be one or the other.

So I went to the cottage which was ten miles from here, and it was the most beautiful place that I ever lived in, besides this house, an absolutely lovely place, a lovely, lovely setting and I really gathered myself there for the year. I suppose it was a jumbled up year. I wasn't sure I had done the right thing or that I was doing the right thing. It was the first time I had ever lived on my own. I didn't feel guilty because I wasn't living a farce. I wasn't going in there in the evening performing, and I really didn't want to perform any more. I have a certain level of faith now and I don't have to be institutionalised, and yet we all have commitments no matter what life we lead.

After less than the year, I knew I wasn't going to go back. I had the letter written to Rome and all business done because I knew it was right. I think writing the letter made me feel good. I didn't want to leave that cottage. I wanted to stay there because it was the most beautiful place that I had ever stood in.

I wrote a lovely letter to them to say I wasn't going to go back and they answered promptly. When my annulment came back from Rome they asked me would I like to come up and sign it. They had a lovely prayer service for me. Just as the prayer started it poured rain and the thunder and lightening came and I said, 'I wonder is that a sign?' My Novice Mistress and a girl who entered with me came down to the cottage for tea and we had a lovely evening, and that was the hardest evening since I left and the most confusing evening. Even though I knew I had made the right decision it was the loneliness. Now I can allow people to do things for me and lots and lots of people are doing things for me and it's wonderful.

In religious life I didn't come first

Talking has brought up stuff in my life now, how I react to people and what I'm learning and will always be learning is that I sometimes come first, and in religious life I didn't come first. I put everyone else first and it was drilled into us in 1972, from 1972 onwards. It was drilled into us. We were to be selfless. You were meant to do extra for others and not consider yourself. Since I left I found that quite a thing.

When I lived in the community the nuns didn't go out very often and they didn't have the sense of dress to go out. When I left I had to relearn the stuff I had done years ago, no, not relearn, learn how to do it properly. For instance, going into a restaurant and reading a menu. I have accomplished that with great glee. I'm absolutely delighted. I can go in and choose. I'm very clear on what I choose, on what I want and how I want it, and if it doesn't suit me I can say it.

The other thing is buying clothes. It was an absolute nightmare because I didn't know how to do it. I didn't know what to buy because I didn't know what went with what, even though I had bought for children. What would suit me, trying to make out my own identity in the way I present myself? I think that is what I was doing and I didn't know. I suppose I still am. I haven't yet the same confidence I have about eating out. The other thing, I suppose, is being honest with myself.

My father died this year. I think that now in these months that he's very real or that I am expecting to go and visit him. I'm not going and I'm wondering why I'm not going. I feel I should be going. He had MRSA and because I was getting treatment I couldn't go to see him. He knew I was ill. In the last few weeks I have been thinking about him a lot. I'm just getting on with life and enjoying it, and if there's anything going on I'm ready for it.

You don't fit into the regime any more

Did I tell you about teaching the sister to drive? It's about the twenty-ninth year and she's still learning to drive! She rang me and said she had no one to accompany her. She's there and she's frustrated out of her mind. She's dealing with a lot of elderly sisters. She lets the frustration out when she goes out in the car. She talks about it and all I do is listen to her. It reminds me of how I was. It's exactly the same. When she's talking, I can feel how I was before I left, the whole frustration of it. My head, I couldn't be listening to them! Did it matter whether the jam or the marmalade was on the table? The world is falling apart and we're dealing with God knows what all day and we come home to this and I think why are they doing this? Where are they now and where am I? And the divide was too wide. I couldn't bring myself back to it. Listening to her brings it all up for me. It tells me how I felt and it tells me I don't feel like that anymore. So it tells me I'm in the right place.

And when I go in and listen to them I think, what are you doing? I don't know what they are doing. There's no work to do in the house, only clean it and tidy it. You don't need to do that all day. There's voluntary work and there are refugees there to be entertained in the sense of a cup of tea and talking to them but there's none of that. They could be active; they are healthy people. I'm looking at them and they're the nicest of people. They give me the greatest of welcome but I say thank God I'm going home to Muffin (the cat) and the house and whatever else I'm going to do.

Well, they're doing the best they can, I suppose. The community I left has become very small and the majority of them have now retired. I visited it recently and I just wonder where they are going now that they are not active enough to work. What are they doing with their time? They have no time to do anything because they are busy. What are they busy about? Is it putting the cups straight and keeping the knives and forks straight? It's nearly a reverse back to the past because they're not active outside the community. What are they doing? They're minding tea towels and putting out teacups. Where's all the enthusiasm? They're losing it. They've lost it.

I have great trust in those doctors. I have trust in those nurses who take time to talk to me. And I have a great trust in God because this is my journey and nobody can be on my journey but me. I wonder had leaving the convent anything to do with the illness? I'm sure people would say, 'If she stayed where she was it wouldn't have happened to her. If she didn't go she wouldn't have had all that stress on her, she wouldn't be stressed.' There's no stress in the convent, you must know that! Do you know it gives me the feeling that they think it's the person that is at fault? This may be wrong but I think you leave because you don't fit into the cog any more. You don't fit into the regime any more. So therefore there must be something wrong with you. It's as if everything is all right here but there's something wrong with you. And they don't look at the here and now and what might stop you leaving. Some of them don't have the courage to come out of the convent, or they think it's too late, and I don't think it's too late. It's never too late to do anything and I think that people who are there now would wish that they could go.

You could feel a bit cheated

It was too closed for me. I had great laughs and I still have some of those friends. Getting sick was hard. I was just getting going. I could feel a bit cheated. I love Friday evenings. I'm starting to read things now and I'm starting to come out from under the study. I'm able to do gardening and I'm able to do things that are relaxing. I'm becoming relaxed in myself and I'm thinking of my next holiday, which may be in October some time after I've walked up the middle of the hall with the high shoes and the noise.

I believe there is a call but sometimes the journey changes and I feel I'm called to do something different now, and while I'm still doing the same work I'm giving myself to people in work and in friendship.

10

Becky

'The way of life was actually killing me'

Introduction

Becky is now forty-six. She came from a typical Irish family that had a welcome for all. The family gatherings were joyful affairs where games were played, songs were sung and stories exchanged. Becky has three siblings. She has a less than satisfactory relationship with her mother, which she attributes to her mother's history around the time of Becky's birth.

As a young couple her parents emigrated to England but they continued to move back and forth between the two countries. Her uncle established a machinery business in Essex and the couple intended to be part of the business. When Becky's maternal grandfather became ill the family moved back to Ireland to look after him. Becky and her sister were born there. Her grandfather died some days after her birth, and the uncle who came from Essex to arrange the funeral died and was buried days before his father. This affected Becky's mother quite intensely and not least her relationship with Becky. Following these events the family return to England and started over.

Becky was involved in her local church and got to know the nuns in the convent near her home. They asked her to be a com-

panion to their novice and she became closer to the nuns, often praying and eating with them. At the time she was working in an office and she got the idea she would like to do something more, so at twenty-one years of age, she decided to become a nun. She had an image of nuns as naïve and cruel. This image originated with her mother who saw the nuns who had taught her in Ireland as cruel, vindictive, ungodly and known for beating children. Becky thought she could dispel that image for others.

Before starting her novitiate she spent some happy times in a convent with older nuns, in their eighties, who told her tales of the past when they sent novices out to water dry sticks, something they now regretted. Later, in another convent for the elderly, they regaled her with tales of the past and made her feel at home.

Her first feelings in the community house to which the novitiate was attached were of an immense heaviness and unhappiness. Perhaps this was how the nuns in this house felt. She continued to feel unhappy, in spite of her resolution to succeed, and she did not become institutionalised by internalising the social defence system of 'no feeling'. The nuns did not, or were unable, to acknowledge their feelings; instead they 'acted out' as did the nun who sat on Becky because she was sitting in what she had appropriated as her chair. In her mind, Becky did not exist so she could sit on her with impunity. Metaphorically, this could be interpreted as this nun's unconscious desire to 'sit on' Becky by curbing her, and bringing her into line with her own wishes. Becky felt the isolation and rejection intensely.

Becky did not like many other aspects of the immature behaviour of these nuns. It is not surprising that these nuns were incapable of acting in a mature, adult manner. They probably entered in their late teenage years with little experience of life in the world, and the convent did not provide the containment necessary to manage feelings of any kind. New, young members who showed their enthusiasm became easy targets for the resentment and antagonism that these disgruntled nuns felt towards those who faced them with the demands of cultural change.

Becky's dislike of the opulent surroundings in which the majority of this middle class order lived contrasted with the life she had lived up until now and her identification with the lay sisters, many of whom were Irish. The practice of having lay sisters was ended after Vatican II, but the scars of this class distinction remained in those who had been the victims of this system and there was no change in the allocation of work. Becky sees the change as cosmetic, that changing the title did little to redress the balance of injustice.

The nuns' lack of understanding of the difficult work that Becky did as a social worker, and the extra demands that were put on her, made her life difficult. She was closer to her work colleagues than to the nuns with whom she lived. She thought the order had strayed from its mission to the poor and the founder's vision for her nuns. Becky was not aware of the pre-Vatican II life the nuns had lived. By clinging to old habits, they were attempting to provide continuity and trying to convince themselves that nothing has changed. It is no less understandable that younger people, fresh from a different society, with a different expectation of religious life, find this way of life intolerable.

Living in the world required new financial arrangements, and by the early 1990s nuns were receiving a monthly allowance and money for holidays. This allowed them to travel abroad. Becky was surprised that the nuns got money for holidays, but yet she felt happy enough to be able to pay her way. However, this holiday had a rather paradoxical outcome because, although Becky seemed happy with the money, it was on this holiday that she decided to leave the convent. She had desired to live simply and without much money, and it was in the freedom of the holiday that she realised that this life was not for her.

Becky did not become institutionalised in the convent, but she had a somewhat idealistic view of elderly nuns from Ireland and she forgave them their earlier acts of cruelty on novices in their charge because they were honest and regretted what they had done. Her social conscience could not condone her middle-class order's treatment of the lay sisters nor their mission to wealthier pupils. She threatened the status quo by wishing to live a spiritual life in a group of people who worked for the poor. She became disillusioned and she returned to the world with the utmost sadness at having failed in her self-appointed task of changing her mother's image of nuns, and with her dream of a shared spiritual life in the convent, helping the less fortunate, shattered.

Becky's Story:

I got in contact with the nuns in the early eighties because their novitiate house was just down the road, in our local parish. I was involved in the music group and I was asked to befriend one of the novices, Maria, because she was around my age. So I got to know her and that meant popping into the convent and picking her up and going off walking or whatever. I used to go and have a meal sometimes with the nuns or go to prayers. We didn't do very much really. We just palled around like young people do and it gradually came to my asking myself what's stopping me from doing this? I always felt I needed to do something more than just working in an office, and so gradually I decided I would give it a go. I was twenty-one. So I said to the nuns, 'I'd really like to try this'.

They sent me off for psychological testing and I came back absolutely floored by that. I had to go and see a guy, a priest, in London and I was just completely devastated by the kinds of things he was saying about me. He said, and he denied it afterwards but I know he said it, something like, 'you are a spineless jellyfish that clings on to people', and that I did things to please other people. He was just asking loads of questions like, 'What do you like most? What do you hate most? What is the best thing about your mother? What's the best thing about your father?' Then he basically said, 'You hate your mother, or you are too ambivalent towards her'. My mother and I didn't have a very good relationship. So what? I was in my early twenties. I was working. I'd got a job. I'd got loads of friends.

I went to see him twice. I had to drive back home after it. I was crying all the way home I was so upset by what he had said and I went to the convent and I said to the nuns, 'I don't want anything to do with this, if this is what it is, it's cruel, you know this is terrible'. And one of the nuns was so upset she rang him and he said he didn't say any of that. You don't make up something like this when you have no experience of psychotherapists or analysts. Why would you sit, as a twenty-two-year-old and come back and say he said this if he didn't say it? It affected me for quite a while.

I knew that there were issues with my Mum because of her history, my birth and everything. I knew that would always be something, but of the four of us children I'm the only one who has tried to understand her. She lost her Mum at the age of twelve and she lost her father the week I was born. Within days of my being born, she'd lost a father and a brother. The two of them died. The brother had come over to Ireland the week that I was born to organise his father's funeral and his own funeral took place before his father's. He was only thirty-nine years of age. So when it comes to my birthday in September my mother is looking out the window going, 'Oh, it was raining like this on the day of the funeral'. There was nothing good happening at that time. That's my story with her.

This psychologist said I'd have difficulty with authority. I told the nuns he damages people. I felt he knocked me to pieces and I was left putting myself back together again. I've got this theory about it. He was a very attractive, very handsome priest, and I think the nun who sent me to him fancied him, had a crush on him. I think he used his sexuality to be brutal. I was sobbing in the car coming back from this therapy session where he gave his conclusions about the kind of character that I was. So I went to the convent in tears. I didn't even tell my family about it. I went to the nuns and I said this bloke has just torn me to pieces and they said, 'Look do you want to come and try it out? You're going to have to move from here, we're going to have to move the novitiate if you join us. You are too close to home.' So my Mum and Dad were devastated. My Mum didn't speak to me for a month and my Dad found it so difficult to think that I'd be moving away. At that time if we joined we wouldn't be able to go home for a year. That was in 1982.

I started my novitiate

I went to one of the convents belonging to the order and spent a few months there before starting my novitiate. I just loved it. I loved the chapel and I loved all the sisters. They were the older generation. They were in their eighties, wise owls and sorry, as well, about a lot of the stuff they had done when they were younger. They would tell me how they sent novices out to water dry sticks to test their obedience and all that stuff. And I used to sit, fascinated by them, fascinated by their lives.

September came and the novitiate had been set up. It was a community house that they made into the novitiate. I don't know if it was especially for me. So all the novices for the next few years went to this house. I started my novitiate and it was really strange because as soon as I walked into this community I felt this immense heaviness over me. I just knew as soon as I got there that I'd be so unhappy and I was. It was the unhappiest house I have ever been in.

After a year and a half I had to do my twenty-eight day retreat before I made first vows. So I went to Wales and it was an amazing experience. It rooted me in spirituality and a feeling that life was always too complicated, even in religious life it was too complicated, it needed to be much simpler.

There was nobody in the order who was a social worker

I was asked, 'What are you going to do? Are you going to teach or what are you going to do after novitiate? We need you to decide what you want to do. We want you to teach.' I said, 'I don't want to teach. I don't think I could do it, what about social work?' They said it was a teaching order, that there was nobody who was a social worker. Everything around the day was based on teachers. So that isolated me from everybody else. So I was a bit of a strange fish for them in what I was doing anyway.

I found that sisters of a certain age were very selfish people. I was staying in a community and attending a local college doing A levels because I didn't have enough qualifications to do the social work course. I was going in to watch an Irish match. I think it might have been a boxing match, Barry McGuigan. I sat down and one of the sisters came in and just sat on my knee because I was sitting in her chair. So I had to move and I remember sitting on the little pouffe by the door watching this boxing match thinking, well, that's it. I'm isolated again from the rest of the community. So much for my aspirations! I think they thought that young people have all these aspirations about a way of life that is completely unrealistic. The way of life more than spirituality I think. When I look at it now I ask why are they living an individual life in sheltered housing somewhere? What's that all about? So I don't know, I don't know.

When I first did my course in social work it was a two-year course. We had to go on placement to various places as part of the qualification. One such placement was an office in the middle of a shopping arcade. So it was really, really busy and on my first day at this placement the team leader looked me up and down because I was there dressed a bit like this really. I didn't know what to wear to be honest. So I was in jeans and a jumper and she looked me up and down and she went, 'Oh, oh right, that's okay then'.

'What do you mean?'

'I thought you'd be in a long flowing frock and a big veil, I don't know how the people in this area would take to it.'

She'd obviously got these pre-conceived ideas about what I would be like and I think I was more of a shock to her than the team were to me to be honest. On another placement a woman said to me, 'I was taught by nuns when I was a child and I didn't know they had feet'.

'What do you mean?'

'Because they had these long flowing dresses on, you never saw their feet, you just thought they floated along the ground.'

So I just spent years, years and years and years trying to describe my life to those who didn't know anything about it.

Has she had a stroke?

I was going to tell you that story about the champagne. I qualified as a social worker in 1989 and that summer we were having a novices' meeting in Dublin. There were about sixteen or eighteen of us, from England and Ireland. It was great for us because we saw a whole different lifestyle. There were probably about five of us altogether in England, Wales and Scotland. I bought this bottle of champagne on my education grant and I took it with me all the way over to Dublin. I wanted to share it because the young nuns had become really good friends, and we'd be out kicking football, letting off steam, in the evenings when the lectures were finished. I got this bottle of champagne out and they went mad. Well, the Novice Mistress in Dublin went mad. I went to our Novice Mistress and I said, 'I can't believe it. There are about twenty-four of us. We wouldn't even have a mouthful each of this stuff and they are terrified we were all going to turn into alcoholics.' I couldn't believe it.

So that was one cracker of an incident and another one was much later when I was assistant superior in a community in the south. There were probably about eight of us. We all came to the table to eat and this nun was slurring her words and falling over and dropping everything. She was dropping her food and dropping her knives and fork and the superior looked at me and she said, 'Has she had a stroke?' I said, 'Are you joking, there's nothing wrong with her except she's probably drunk a bottle of the altar wine'. She was absolutely flutered on this altar wine so she went to bed for the rest of the evening. I just thought it was quite funny because these nuns were still very naïve about the world and they were very protective of us younger ones when we probably knew more about it all than they did.

They thought they were the elite squad

I really wondered if some of these middle aged nuns who were in their forties when I was in my twenties were quite threatened by younger people coming in and wanting to change things and wanting to bring a new spirit to the order. They just seemed to be so selfish and they thought they were the elite squad. A cohort of them from the same college had joined around the same time. I don't know what their motivation was. I think they purposely made life very difficult for others but there was a whole bunch of them anyway, a whole mob around the same age. They joined within a few years of each other and they'd all gone to the same school and then there were some siblings among them. There was one particular pair and they thought they were the foundation stone of the order. That's what their mother had said of them. She said that the order was lucky to have them because they'd be two of the foundation stones of the order. They lived within a few miles of each other and one of them was in my community.

In all the communities when you have a car you share it and look after it. This nun would book the car for every day of the year as soon as the new diary came in. She would put her name by the car every single day of the year so that nobody else would be able to have it. There were probably two cars in the community at the time. She would drive this car from the community to go and see her sibling who was based about nine miles away. They would then get in one of her sister's community cars and drive away. So one car would be left on the drive and that would stop anyone from that community using that car for the weekend. This particular nun used to communicate with me on yellow sticky notes that she'd leave on the table in the hallway.

When I was training she would use her car to drive to the chaplaincy at the university, which was on the bus route from the community house, and it would be parked out there all day because she wouldn't be going anywhere else. She would never ever consider that I could use it instead of getting three buses every morning. It was all part of my learning and humility to get on three buses. Apparently I could sit and write notes on the bus. I think it was just control.

She also reported me to a member of the provincial council for something. I can't remember what I did, took a car without permission or something. One day the two of them were sitting in the front room and I just laid into them. I was just so angry and I said to this woman that she didn't have any respect for anyone or anything and, 'if this is what community life is about then you can stuff it'. They were a bunch of control freaks, particularly in that community. At that time there were probably about eight of us in that house, it was huge, it was massive, and it probably had about twelve bedrooms.

The attitude to us novices was, you are here living free, so get out and do stuff. We had to do it, so you will do it. We did all the nasty jobs because we had to earn our living somehow. I'd be sent on all these weekend retreats with kids who didn't want to be on them. They'd be hiding the Vodka in the bags and then getting drunk and it was freezing cold in these retreat houses. We just stood in for the other nuns because it was something we could do to help. We were not really earning, not really contributing to the community.

It's your turn, so off you go

I stayed in this house during term time while I was training and then in holiday times I used to go out to Wales. It was a retirement home so I was spending time again with all the nuns in their eighties and nineties who told stories about when they entered. One of them told me that she was out in the fields in Ireland cutting the hay with her family and her sister was asked if she wanted to go to the convent and she said 'no', and so the parents turned to this one, Mary Kate, and said, 'Right Mary Kate, she won't go, it's your turn, so off you go'. And she left and joined the order.

The stories that we'd have and the fun that we'd have! I just loved the older Irish nuns. I loved their wisdom. I loved their simplicity of life and the ones I got on with were those who would be peeling the spuds and cooking the dinners and cleaning and mopping the floors. I had nothing in common with the intellectuals, the teachers, at all. A whole crowd of us would just sit around the table with the oranges making the marmalade and jams. They were special to me, probably because of my upbringing in an Irish household.

The links with Ireland were really strong

In our house, at home, the door was never locked. Nobody made appointments to see anybody. We'd all, my uncles and aunties, have singsongs. We'd be in the sitting room playing cards or everyone had to do a turn. We'd sing a bit of a song or tell a story. We were brought up on tales of their childhood. The links with home and Ireland were just really strong.

My Mum's father died the week I was born. My parents were coming over to Essex to join my Mum's older brother to work. He had started some kind of machinery business and sadly he died the week after I was born. My Granddad had died three days earlier. My Mum and Dad had come over to England when they were younger and had kept going back home. My mother's mother had died when she was a child and so my Granddad had brought up twelve of them working for the council in the south of Ireland. My Dad came over when he was a teenager. Then he met my Mum. He became a Catholic to marry her. As my Granddad was getting more and more ill my Mum and Dad went back to Ireland and lived with him until he died. My sister and I were born in Ireland and then after he died they came back to Essex. All the plans for this big business were shelved because my uncle had died. So they had to start from nothing really.

They would fuss over the priests

I just couldn't reconcile the convent lifestyle to the way I'd been brought up. We didn't have anything and I had gone from being a working class student at secondary school and not doing very well to living this middle class lifestyle, the china in the cupboards and all the rest of it. I would just walk around these parlour rooms and look at all this furniture and stuff and think I don't want this! I don't want this! There was this huge chapel in one convent and I always used to say to the community there that it was very minimalist, but minimalist in the most ostentatious way that you could. The furniture was all made of fabulous oak and it was such a contradiction to me. They had spent thousands and thousands on this chapel and I just thought what's that all about, what is it for, why are all these thousands of pounds being spent on something like this? And buying cars! It was just all beyond me! It was all beyond me! I didn't want any of it.

There was a girl from Sussex I'd known for years and she'd come on the same retreat as us. She had picked us up and dropped us in her car at the retreat house and then dropped us back. I said to her, 'Well, come in and have lunch with us, there's always an extra plate in our house'. I was lambasted for not making an appointment, for not telling the nuns that this girl was coming. She didn't even get a cup of tea, nothing, not even a glass of water. I had invited her in unbeknown and they were all mad, because I hadn't rung them to ask. It's like my whole history is why. We are supposed to be inviting people in. She had to go to drop us at the gate and drive off.

The way they would fuss over the priests used to drive me mad. They would flirt with all these priests. It just made me laugh. I remember being asked if I would be a minister of the Eucharist, you know, of communion, and I said, 'I'm not really bothered, I don't really mind', and this priest said to me, 'If you are going to do this you've got to put your veil on', and I said to him, 'I'm not doing it then', because we didn't wear veils at the time and I said, 'No I'm not bothering then. There are loads of other people in the parish who might want to do this.' I didn't want to do it. The first day I was given a veil was at my reception and half way through the party thing, you know, the tea and cakes afterwards,

I took the veil off and hung it on the chair and I never wore it since. I don't know where it went actually.

I worked for ten years as a social worker

When I qualified as a social worker I was looking for jobs. I went for an interview and I got the job in London and worked and lived there for ten years. I commuted every day, went to Mass in the parish church before I started work, whereas the rest of the community were all at Mass in the convent chapel before school started. It was all geared towards the teachers. I used to come in at six o'clock at night and the food was there on the table ready. I was just walking in the door as they were sitting down to eat and even now I find it so difficult to walk in and eat. I have to have some time before I have my tea or dinner or whatever.

I hate having a Sunday dinner because it was an established thing in the community that we'd have to take turns cooking and we'd be cooking Sunday dinner for fourteen people, and if someone had guests coming there might be sixteen or eighteen people around this huge table. You'd spend the whole day preparing the food and cooking it, and then the day would be gone and you'd be back to work on Monday morning.

There isn't a convent there now. They sold it off. They got millions for it. There were two great big five-storey terraced houses in London with interconnecting doors on each floor. They were separate communities but they came together for different things. It was a base for all the visiting nuns from all over the world. I'd come in from work and I'd see all these suitcases at the bottom of the stairs. I'd know that all we'd be doing would be making beds and running a B&B! I'd be doing my job at work and I'd be criticised for going to bed early. And I'd be saying I'm doing child protection work. I do child abuse. I'm not running a B&B here, and I felt they had no understanding of the pressures of my job whatsoever.

For the first time I was respected

Once I was happy living in a community in London in one of these big houses. There were six of us in this community and the oldest was in her eighties, I was the youngest and Antonia was the superior. She was a singer, a musician so gifted and I loved her to bits. She used to ask my opinion about things, 'Do you think we should do this, Becky? Do you think we should go here? Do you think it's right?' Whatever decision was made as a community I used to be included in it. I felt a part of it. Augustine was the oldest and she was great fun. On St. Patrick's Day she'd come down in this hat and a dress and have shamrock for all of us. For the first time I was respected as a part of the community, not just a novice or someone in the novitiate that is sucking off the whole institute because that was how they made you feel a lot of the time.

The community in my parish where I lived with my parents seemed to me to be a really exciting group of people in the sense of they were almost liberated. They were out with the community, working with people there. The opportunity of working with people was immense. You get really get to work with the poor in whatever way they were poor – physical, psychological, emotional whatever – and that's what I dreamed of doing because our founder was such an exciting character. She had great faith. Her life was fantastic, amazing.

It was a kind of double life

In my own way, in my job with my work friends and colleagues, I gave them a bit of an insight into how I lived my life. But then my life was very different from the life the others lived in the same house so it was all a bit strange really. I'm surprised I'm not a bit more cracked. It was this kind of double life. I was on the edge of two worlds all the time, and neither life was fulfilling me at all. I felt I wanted to live a simple life in community with other like-minded people but nobody really felt like that within the community. I wanted to live the life that the founder wanted for her nuns, to live in companionship and to work with the poor and to teach people about the faith in whatever way that was.

I wondered if people purposely make their religious life more complicated, or have I got a simplistic attitude about it? I didn't quite know. I didn't have any nun as a work colleague. I didn't feel that anybody understood what I was about at all.

I felt misunderstood, particularly when I was doing the child care social work. I'd be involved in a lot of difficult abuse cases or I would know of them. I would come back to the community and they would be arguing about who left the bread out of the bread bin the night before, or who left the butter knife in the butter, or who should put the labels on the cupboard doors? Oh God, it is all the stupid things that community life is about.

'Who is going to clean the bath?'

'Well, it's not my job.'

'Who is going to do the shopping this week?'

'Oh, I'm not bothered.'

'I'll do it. I'll do the shopping.'

The priorities for me were very different. It's not surprising that they didn't understand it. I might want to go for a drink with my friends or go to the pictures or go for a walk on Hampstead Heath with good friends I had made from work and that's all it was. I had to explain my life away. I thought it's too restrictive. I'm not living my vows the way I want to live. I thought I'm going to become a really old and twisted nun if I don't do something about this.

I was based in a house that was worth hundred of thousands at the time. And they would say, 'Let's have a decorator in to paint'. And I would think, my parents never got a decorator in to paint. I was taught how to paint because we needed it. Nobody in her right mind would get a decorator in. So I would be saying, 'Why get a decorator in, I can do that wall? Get the paint and I'll do it.'

'No, no we're giving a poor man a job.' That was the attitude, we're giving him work to do or else he wouldn't have any work would he? There was a patronising attitude towards people. We'll do this for you because you are poor, you need the money.

It was met with silence

What I found quite upsetting were the lay sisters. It was the community nuns and the lay sisters. It was the lay sisters who didn't have a teaching qualification who were in the kitchens and did the laundry and the cleaning. I remember being at a provincial meeting and one of these sisters saying how much she hated being a lay sister because she always felt a second-class citizen within the order. Some sisters were teaching, or being headmistresses, while all the lay sisters were doing was washing their underwear. There was a big gap in the responsibilities and I think that a lot of the older lay sisters felt that discrimination quite deeply. I remember being at a provincial meeting and I wrote a poem about this nun who sat opposite me crying. She was in her seventies and she still hadn't got over how she was treated as a lay sister within the order. She cried her heart out about the injustice of her life. It was met with silence, silence. That memory stayed with me forever because it was just heart wrenching, the anger and upset she had to endure all her life.

After Vatican II the title went

I've come from a relatively poor Irish family who had nothing and I will have nothing left to me. I'm not from a privileged family so everything that I saw around me just seemed so opulent and big, and the community nuns were probably from quite wealthy middle-class families. Well, the lay sisters were mostly from Ireland. I suppose that's why I got on better with them because they were like my family. After Vatican II we went back to the original charism of the founder and the title went. They weren't called lay sisters any more, they were all sisters but they all had different jobs. It didn't mean enough. Our nuns were frightfully middle class and the Irish used to call themselves their country cousins. Then moving to England they considered themselves the bumpkins.

I felt that part of that exclusive club of being a community nun is still there in some way, and particularly in those who lorded it over everyone because they were quite a strong group of people, quite opinionated, and they could effect change. A group of like-minded people like that could either stop progress or continue progress, but I don't know what they were up to really. I couldn't quite work it out. I never thought about people's motivations. I just wanted to focus on where I was in all this and how I was going to serve God.

Yet there were so many of them that I did respect. They were wise old women who had been through it all and change wasn't fazing them. Change wasn't easy for them but they didn't question it that much. It was one group of people of middle age who seemed to think this order would not survive without them. They thought that they were superior to everybody else to the point of excluding people.

A lot more freedoms

After Vatican II they developed this whole different way of life that was much freer. People could wear their own clothes and it was much more of an open lifestyle in the sense of doing a lot more, a lot more freedom. I think it was that the middle-aged group saw us as a threat to their lifestyle, to the way they had developed their community life. A few of us came in saying we wanted to live a simple lifestyle. A lot of these nuns would have been very young, sixteen or seventeen when they entered.

The older nuns who were mother superiors in the 1960s when these younger women had joined would say to me openly, 'We were cruel, we made such terrible decisions for these young people and now we are eighty, ninety and we can sit back and think'. Some of them took on the changes, but to them the importance was living community life with each other in their old age.

I feel there was no coherent development after Vatican II. It was all jumbled up. Everyone was doing different things all over the place. I think Vatican II definitely made life more complicated because there was no direction for anybody. I only experienced it afterwards. I don't know how long the transition took. Nobody left. They moved out and lived on their own. Well, as far as I know one nun left and she came back two years later. She moved out completely and then came back. When I left she was the provincial. She took two years out to decide. Her sibling left as well but she never came back.

I think I shocked them

By the time I left there weren't so many teaching. They had private schools. I remember they had a schools' meeting because they wanted to decide what direction they wanted to be moving in and I went along. I said, 'I'm not a teacher, why do you want me to be there because I don't know anything about teaching'. They were congratulating themselves on what fantastic schools they had, on what a fantastic job they were doing with all these girls around the country, all these footballers paying top whack for private schools for their kids, that discipline wasn't a problem. It was making me madder and madder. I said, 'What do you do with those girls who feel like they are the shit in the gutter?' And they were mortified because I used the word 'shit' to start with and I could hear them all going 'ahhh' with an intake of breath. Then I said, 'What do you do? What do you do with those kids who feel like they're nobody, have nothing?' It just all went dead. I used to pop in those kinds of questions. I often wondered if anybody that they taught become socially aware or are they just the elite in society now? I think I shocked the nuns. Those who were intellectuals, and some of them were superiors and headmistresses, and they had no idea of how to deal with young people or with other members of the community. Some of them had a common sense approach. I think they had just forgotten about poor people. They had become so far removed from them.

I work with the people who have failed, who are seeing themselves as nothing, as worthless, as tramps, as drunks, as drug addicts. I don't see any success in what I do. Once we were having a session about sharing about our jobs and I talked about the people who don't necessarily change their lives in a positive way. All I can do is be with them during that time.

Cruel, vindictive and ungodly altogether

I purposely wanted to dispel the whole image of what nuns were in the sense of naïve but cruel. My mother saw the image of the nuns who taught her in Ireland as being cruel and vindictive and ungodly altogether. It was common knowledge that they were brutal, that they used to beat. That was her experience of them. So I went out of my way to be somebody that isn't anything like that. I would go for drinks with my friends and they'd say to me, 'You are having a glass of beer, you shouldn't be doing that should you?'

'But why not, what's wrong with that? What's wrong with having a glass of wine?'

'Nothing wrong with it!'

So I spent my working life as a nun just dispelling all the preconceived ideas about what I should be and what I shouldn't be and who I was. I loved that. I loved having conversations with people who knew nothing about religious life because I could tell them, 'Well, no, actually, nuns can be the most selfish bitches you can ever meet in your life and it's not Julie Andrews and *The Sound of Music* at all in any way, shape or form'. I'd love to tell people what motivates me, what I want to do and why I want to do it, but never felt that anybody understood that within the community. I just found it a very selfish life, and when I explained that to people who weren't Catholic or Christian they were just really shocked. When I spoke to my family or friends, my parents, my brother and my sisters, my cousins, my best friends from home here and from Ireland who were Catholic, they weren't shocked at all.

I might as well leave

I just remember that nun who cried and how angry she was at how she had lived her life, and the disrespect she had had from the other nuns. I always thought of her. I'm going to end up like her if I stay because I'm going to be so angry about it. I knew that I was isolated. I didn't know that it was loneliness. I knew I did something different and the nuns saw me as doing something different.

I remember the Mother General came for meetings and I was meant to see her. At the time I had moved from childcare into adult work, working with people with disabilities and old people. On this day I had to do this emergency admission and I was late back to this meeting with the general. I was just completely exhausted and she went into this entire thing, 'Was I happy?'

I couldn't stop crying, 'I don't know what I'm doing, I don't know what I'm doing here', and I just felt I was living on the edge of two lives all the time. I was finding that my main support network were people I worked with and not people I lived with. It was only when I left that I discovered that I had been so lonely living in a community of people. I was lonelier there than I was living on my own. It was a gradual thing. I never wanted to go, never wanted to leave. I really did want to make final vows and that be for life. But I just felt that people had so many personal agendas about how they wanted to live religious life and they were beginning to be living in sheltered housing, on their own in flats, three or four of them in a sheltered housing block, all living in separate flats on their own. And I thought, where's the community in that? Where's the sisterhood? I might as well leave and do it myself. I might as well do that myself and do it in my own way without any restrictions from anybody, and it took me a while to decide but I think it was the isolation and the loneliness. I eventually think that I did make the right decision to leave because I was so unhappy. I just couldn't reconcile myself to the way people were living, and I know that I would have become bitter and twisted and been like the worst kind of old nun. By 1993, I had had enough.

Money for holidays

In the early nineties everybody got a sum of money to go on holiday, a couple of hundred quid. Here we were living on ten pounds a month and then suddenly we were given this amount of money, and at that time we could go all over the place for that. So I went on holiday with my friend, Susan, from work. She wasn't in a relationship at the time and we became really good friends and still are, amazingly good friends. She didn't have any belief in anything, yet she was the one who knew more about my life and understood it more than any of the religious sisters that I lived with. So we went on our holiday and we were on the beach and it was the first time ever that I could even go out for a meal with her and be able to pay my own way. I didn't see any of my earnings apart from the ten pounds a month, and if we went out as a group of friends from work they would always pay for my meal, because I didn't have the money to do it. So for the first time in my life, in my religious life, I was there, we were going out for drinks or whatever, a pizza or meal at night and there I was putting as much in as she was. This got me thinking and we were on the beach in Turkey and I said to her, 'I've got to jump over the wall Susan, I've just got to jump over the wall, I've got to do it and now is the time before it's too late, before I get too old'.

I'm going to live a better life outside

I asked the provincial if I could take some time out. So I moved out of the community. So after the two years I said, 'I'm not coming back, I've decided'. I'm going to live a better life outside. So that is when they agreed for me to have this £5,000 and I used that for a deposit to buy a flat in London and I moved into it. Because I had spent all my adult life in a community of women I thought, I must be odd, I must be strange, and I used to say to my male colleague at work, 'Am I odd, am I weird?'

He said, 'What are you on about?'

'But I've lived for twelve years in a female-orientated environment.'

'You've sat opposite me for three years working with me, how can you be odd?'

'I dunno, talk to men, I don't know how to talk to men, I don't know how to engage with men, I don't know how to speak to them.'

'You've been talking to me for the past three years. What's wrong with you?'

I spent two years trying to get my head around my life and now I actually think I'm dead normal. I've got a great family, I've got a bunch of really supportive friends, there's nothing wrong with me. I met David and we got married, and then we decided that we couldn't live in a one bedroomed flat, it was too small, and the housing market had just boomed. Incredible the prices that were going for flats and houses, so we took a year to decide what to do and I said, 'Would you come to Newcastle with me?' and he said, 'Yeah'. So after a year we decided to come up here and we bought this house. I got a job here in social services and that's where I've been ever since. So we have been here now for ten years.

We lost you

There was a bit of a do at the church just a year or two ago for a nun who was retiring and the provincial came down and we sat talking. I said to her, 'Now I never wanted to leave but I never felt as though anyone ever understood what I was about', and she just said, 'We lost you, didn't we, we lost you, through our ignorance we lost you'. I said, 'I don't know about that really but it wasn't something I ever wanted'.

When David and I got married a few of the nuns came to the wedding, which was lovely and one of them said to me, 'Oh well, at least we educated you, at least you got your social work course, at least we got you through your course'.

'I never wanted to leave, I wanted to commit my life to this, I didn't want to ever leave it, but what's the point in staying when you've got absolutely nothing in common with anyone you're living with.'

'Oh well, at least we educated you.'

I felt quite humiliated by that. They gave me the privilege of being educated. They gave me the opportunity to learn. It felt she was saying, the only reason I was in this order was that I could be educated and escape. That wasn't it. If they only knew that the hardest thing in my life was to leave.

I often have dreams about them, being at a conference or something and all the nuns there and me saying, 'I can't be here, I'm married, I've got David in my life. Why am I here? Why am I doing this?' And they are saying, 'Becky, are you going to come back to us?' This is a regular thing that comes up. I think it's when I get stressed. When I get anxious about my work it comes back to this, 'oh are you going to come back?' And I say, 'Yeah, I'll come back and then I think ooh' and I'm shouting at myself in my dream, 'You can't go back you're married now, it's different'.

I think, in some ways, I broke a mould when I was in there. The order made it so difficult for me to go. The provincial, a lovely woman, said, 'I think you're making this terrible mistake'. I said, 'I know I'm not making a mistake'. That was the hardest thing. After that I unplugged my phone. When the letter came from the Vatican, the indult of departure, my friend brought it to the flat to sign and we both sat in the kitchen and signed the paperwork. There were just so many questions and not enough answers.

Spirituality was done and dusted

There are soul-searching questions about spirituality and I'd never had conversations about that with anyone in the order. Maybe it was just assumed that spirituality was done and dusted. There wasn't a lot of spirituality really. If we were living as a community of spiritual people why were they so cruel to each other? Why was spirituality not the central part of their lives? Why was this nun leaving me yellow post-it notes instead of actually speaking to me? I saw two nuns sit at a kitchen table and turn their backs on each other because they couldn't bear to sit at the same table eating their breakfast. None of it seemed to make sense to me, if we were supposed to be living the spiritual life together. What is it all about then? I couldn't work it out. I had a simple philosophy about my life and nobody seemed to grasp it.

It's such a shrouded life

Strange about the dreams though, isn't it? I worked in another surgery, it's up the road from here actually, and there are two teams of district nurses and they were so funny. They were great fun to be with and they were telling me about going to see a play about nuns and they were all going to hire nuns' outfits to go to it. And I said, 'But not many nuns wear the habits now anyway. You wouldn't even know half the nuns who would be around you.'

'How do you know so much about it?'

'Actually I was a nun for twelve years.'

'No, I can't believe it, can't believe it.'

She burst out laughing and I ended up having to give her a photograph. And if ever I have a conversation with people it is interesting that they don't know anything about nuns; it's still such a shrouded life, a shrouded existence really. I think the sisters made it that way. A lot of them weren't open, or welcoming. I wonder if they felt they had something to hide, because if people actually knew the opulent life that they lived they would be quite disgusted by it. It was a wealthy order. I never wanted to leave but the way of life in religious life was actually killing me. The institution couldn't renew itself because it couldn't cope with difference and that leaves a huge sadness.

Conclusion

The life trajectory of the ten nuns in this book is not entirely separate from my own journey. I had spent years of my life in post-Vatican II times in convents in the Midlands and shorter periods in convents in London, Germany and Austria. It took many hours of therapeutic work to free me from the conditioning of convent life and to hear the nuns' stories with an empathic ear.

I set out to explore twentieth century convent life and to do this I listened to ten nuns recount their life stories over three meetings, each of about one hour's duration, depending on the stamina of the nun and her ability to speak freely about herself. I recorded the interviews and later transcribed them. All of the nuns belonged to active orders and they took vows of poverty, chastity and obedience, and promised to educate and work for those in need and to remain in the convent for life.

In relation to their vocations, there were many reasons for joining, such as wishing to leave Ireland, answering an invitation from a sister, wanting to travel, having the desire to look after children or making a covenant with God to bless one's family. Those wishing to go abroad bowed to pressure from male authorities and remained in Ireland. There was a noticeable lack of an explicit wish to pray and serve God, which may be because there was an implicit understanding in the God-centred, devo-

tional society of the time that one entered a convent to pray and
to do God's work.

Eight of the ten nuns joined the convent in the pre-Vatican
II era and they paint a picture of a life that was almost entirely
cut off from the outside world. The reality of the outside world
was replaced by the reality of the convent so that there was little
chance of reality testing, which means the nuns became out of
touch with the real world. They did not go outside the perim-
eter of the convent complex and they lived with minimal com-
munication with the world. Visits from family and friends were
restricted and the superior read all letters coming in and out.
She was like God and her every wish became a command. Blind
obedience to the superior deprived the individual sister of choice
and relieved her of responsibility for her actions. Nothing ex-
cused disobedience. Disobedience was the sin.

The nuns led a common life, praying, eating, working, sleeping and recreating together without any private space or time.
This encouraged immersion in the group and increased control
over the individual. The common life was intended to eliminate
envy. Constant overwork meant there was little time and mental
space for reflection, which deprived the sisters of a critical function necessary for maturation. The emphasis on work was based
on the maxim that the devil finds work for idle hands, so hands
and minds were always busy. All tasks had to be carried out as
prescribed with no opportunity for initiative. Besides their professional work and their prayers, the nuns did other duties, waxing, washing, scrubbing floors in the convent and the schools,
looking after the elderly in the convent, the boarders in the
school and supervising boarders' study. Silence was the rule at
all times except where speaking was necessary to carry out one's
duties. Speaking was permitted at formal recreation periods and
occasionally at meals.

Trivial things, such as being late for a community exercise, gained an importance far beyond their merit and the nuns daily confessed their minor infringements of the rule and kissed the floor. The observance of details of outward behaviour, in order to avoid the exposure and humiliation of this confession of faults, developed a sense of guilt and worthlessness, even about trivial matters.

The vow of poverty ensured that a lack of financial resources left the individual powerless, dependent and often exposed to neglect and deprivation. Dependence meant that one did not develop the skills required to live in the world. A life of dependence made it almost impossible to leave the convent. Similarly, in the Magdalen homes run by the nuns, when the women left, many returned to the institution. Heat and food were scarce commodities and the elderly nuns often went to bed in the evenings to keep warm. Heat and food are recurrent themes in the lives of the sisters and they represent comfort, nurturance and care, which was always in short supply.

All friendships inside and outside the convent were strictly forbidden. Conversations with priests, who were often the only males around, had to be reported verbatim to the superior. The prohibition on particular friendships meant the destruction of human affections and often led to having no friendships at all, resulting in a shutting down of feelings. The repression of feelings had serious implications for the work of the sisters. The ability to empathise, to walk in the shoes of the other, is necessary to understand how people are feeling and to know what they need. The loss of this ability can lead to unfair and cruel acts on other people. Repressed or split off rage can be displaced unconsciously and directed at subordinates, commonly known as 'kicking the cat instead of the boss'.

There was a hidden social class system in convents. This hierarchy was evident in the seating arrangements in the refectory. At the bottom of the hierarchical ladder were the lay sisters who ate their meals separately, either before or after the community. They wore aprons and other minor differences in the habit, discernible to the observant eye. The novices sat at the bottom tables and did the serving. Higher up were the community nuns on both sides, in order of seniority, and at the top table looking down were the superiors, those in charge. Each one knew her place and what was expected of her. On the surface, everything ran smoothly.

As the nuns' stories unfolded it became clear that there was a system of defences in operation to protect against feelings such as anxiety, anger, sadness, doubt and uncertainty. Some defences are conscious and others unconscious. This system develops as the result of collusive interaction and agreement, often unconscious, between the members of an institution. The form it takes will develop over time and, once in place, it becomes an aspect of external reality. It is then taken for granted by the older members of the institution and the new members must come to terms with it.

Turning a blind eye, knowing and not knowing at the same time, defends against insight. The reason for turning a blind eye is the fear of the truth and a reality that cannot be faced. Laughter was, and still is, used as a way of denying feelings of anger, embarrassment and sadness. This is sometimes conscious and is seen as a way of surviving. Conformity as a means of avoiding anxiety is unconscious. It defends against any anxiety that might arise through the operation of conscience. Conscience, the use of judgement and free will were superseded by obedience to the will of the superior. Attacking one's intelligence or blaming oneself, rather than the institution, means the institution is always right and beyond scrutiny. Wrongdoing was seen as personal and the individual felt shame and blamed herself and continued to strive for perfection. Self-censorship is still very strong and the fear of saying too much results in the sister quickly recanting or suddenly saying the opposite, as if she will be punished for speaking her mind.

There was huge pressure to conform. Conformity ensured that the rules were kept because it was of great importance to be in good standing in the group. Non-conformity was punished and rebellion was quelled. There were various ways of punishing people. Non-conformists were often sent away which, at one time, was a huge shame, or they were sent on the missions. If they stayed they were in danger of being victimised as an example to others not to transgress. One can assume that only the strongest survived. Life was made very difficult for those who defied the rules and they often lived in great fear. Fear was a way of controlling the nuns and this culture of fear extended to the workplace where nuns were able to control those in their care by instilling fear.

There are many possible psychological effects of the closed system on the individual personality. Each sister brought her own past experiences and ego strength to bear on the imposed demands of convent life, and was more or less affected psychologically by them. In trying to conform to the system it is likely that the normal maturation process to psychological adulthood became thwarted. Many of the nuns are aware that the system has had a damaging affect on them, but no one links it with how they might have acted as a result. At this stage awareness is more connected to cognition than consequence. They do not look at the effect of immaturity on the work of the institution.

Adults need to be psychologically mature to manage their own anxieties, in order to detoxify and make manageable the anxious feelings of the children in their care.[25] Where an adult cannot process the feelings of her own early deprivation evoked by looking after deprived children, she is likely to abuse these children.[26] In the convent institution, it is possible that there were no mature adults available to fulfil this function. Identification with the aggressor, in this case the harsh convent regime, as aggressor, and the acting out, in violent behaviour, of unacknowledged and unexpressed rage, on less powerful and vulnerable women and children, are also possible outcomes of the oppressive convent regime.

Each one of the eight sisters who entered before Vatican II speaks of her teaching with love and she found solace and satisfaction in her contact with the children. Some saw it as an escape from the strict convent life. This begs the question of the lay sisters and others who were not trained and worked with the most vulnerable. Where did they find their consolation and escape?

The system had to be maintained both inside and outside the convent. In the convent, the lay sisters, and others who were without education or professional training, carried out the domestic duties and worked in the less prestigious laundries and industrial schools. These sisters were often the most vulnerable, carrying out the most difficult tasks. In a system where perfection was the aim, there was no place for the expression of feelings of vulnerability. Those who felt overburdened continued in silence. The teachers and nurses were professionally trained and ensured that the public face of the institution was well represented. This value system was never questioned. There was no thinking in the institution.

The nuns provided social welfare and educational services, in addition to mediation with God through intercessory prayer, to society, in return for good will and sufficient recruits for the continuance of the services. All believed in the teachings of the

Catholic Church and had to uphold its moral standards and be seen to do so. Women who transgressed the strict moral code of the Church were branded as sinners and were removed from society and given into the care of the nuns to make reparation. They were called penitents. The nuns colluded with this. It is likely that these women, the Magdalens, held the projected repressed sexual feelings of the nuns and were then looked upon as bad people. They also held the shadow side of both the nuns and society, including men who were never brought to book for their part in their illicit sexual acts, and had no responsibility for children born as a result. These children too were handed over to the nuns and were possibly looked upon as bad by their association with the Magdalens. They could then be punished with impunity. To be seen as a saint one needs a sinner to offset one's sanctity.

Vatican II (1962–65) called for a humanisation of religious life and an adaptation to the modern world. The special status of religious women was removed, making them equal with, rather than superior to, their lay counterparts. This deprived them of their special function as mediators between God and the laity. In addition, the end of enclosure, and the structures of monasticism, left religious women searching for a new identity.

The two young women, who entered in the 1970s and 1980s, had already finished school and had worked in the world. They came from a different worldview and with very different expectations of religious life. They came from a different background. Both spent their early lives in urban areas in England and neither had been in boarding school, and so they were not so familiar with nuns. They had spent some time working in offices before they decided to enter the convent.

In their early days they found they were dealing with feelings, which, although belonging to them, can also be interpreted as belonging to the older nuns with whom they lived. As a result of the life they had led before Vatican II, these older nuns faced an impossible task when their old defensive ways of living had been exposed. They had great difficulty in adapting. They were psychologically unprepared, and one might say ill equipped, for the challenges that beset them. They retained the mindless activity of the past and often resented younger members. The newcomers were likely receptacles for the projections of these nuns who were were unable to acknowledge their feelings. The feelings were never processed so there was no understanding between the two groups. Both of these young women came into the convent determined to stay, but found they could not tolerate this troubled environment. Their conscious reason for leaving was their inability to straddle two worlds, the old and the new.

More than forty years after Vatican II, the conflict between the institutional mission and the freedom of the individual to choose her own lifestyle and life path continues. Some elderly feel unheld, in freefall, ungrounded. Nothing is set out in stone as it was in the past. Religious life is on the verge of fragmentation. It lacks a unified vision and the commitment essential to its survival. It is too similar to life outside the convent to present a challenge that is appealing to young people. In terms of working for the good of the Church and society, it has nothing extra to offer. It has lost its identity and its function.

Endnotes

1 The words 'nun' and 'sister' are used interchangeably as is the custom in Ireland.

2 Cullen, M. (1987) 'Women, emancipation and politics 1860-1984'. In Cosgrove A. (ed.) *A New History of Ireland* (Vol. II). New York: Oxford University Press, 826-891; Luddy, M. (1995) *Women in Ireland, 1800-1918*. Cork: Cork Univ. Press; MacCurtain, M. (1997) 'Godly burden: The Catholic sisterhoods in twentieth century Ireland'. In Bradley, A. and Valiulis M. (eds.) *Gender and Sexuality in Modern Ireland*. Amherst, Mass: Univ of Mass Press.

3 http://www.socialjustice.ie/sites/default/files/file/catholic-social-thought/chapter6.pdf retrieved 28.07.2014

4 Tovey, H. and Share, P. (2000) *A Sociology of Ireland*. Dublin: Gill and Macmillan.

5 Nic Ghiolla Phadraig, M. (1995) 'The power of the Catholic Church in the Republic of Ireland'. In Clancy, P., Drudy, S., Lynch, K. and O'Dowds, L. (eds.) *Irish Society: Sociological Perspectives*. 593-619. p. 601.

6 MacCurtain, op.cit.

7 Inglis, T. (1998) *Moral Monopoly: The Rise and Fall of the Catholic Church in Ireland*. Dublin: UCD Press.

8 Horgan, G. (2001) *Changing Women's Lives in Ireland*. Online at www.pubs.Socialistreview index. Accessed on 25 August 2008.

9 Mulcahy, T. (2004) 'The new year waits, breathes, waits'. *Religious Life Review*. 43: 345-367.

10 Mulcahy, op. cit.

11 Spence, D. (1982) *Narrative Truth and Historical Truth*. New York: Norton.

12 Moran, F. (2004b) 'To be a religious: Identity and history'. *Religious Life Review*. 43: 301-312.

13 Steiner, J. (1993) *Psychic Retreats*. London: Karnac. p. 93.

14 Steiner, op. cit., p. 129.

15 Steiner, op. cit., p. 116.

16 MacCurtain, op. cit., p. 251.

17 Watkins, A. (2013) *Coherence: The Secret Science of Brilliant Leadership*. USA: Kogan Page.

18 In a Galway convent, the Sister in charge told Halliday Sutherland that the Magdalens took a vow to remain in the Magdalen asylum for life (Sutherland, 1995: 82).

19 Bolognini, S. (2009) 'Real wolves and fake wolves: Alternating between repression and splitting in complex clinical cases'. In Bokanowski, T. and Lewkowicz, S. (eds.) *On Freud's 'Splitting of the Ego in the Process of Defence'*. London: Karnac. 62-83. p. 77.

20 Symington, N. (1994) *Emotion and Spirit*. London: Karnac. p. 101.

21 In the olden days a wren was killed and placed on the top of a pole and the 'wren boys' would carry it around to houses and beg for money to bury the bird, as it was considered to be evil.

22 Slater (1963) 'On Social Regression'. *American Sociological Review*. 28: 339–364. p. 348.

23 Freud, S. (1921) *Group Psychology and the Analysis of the Ego*. SE 18: 65-143. New York: Norton.

24 Coser, L. (1974) *Greedy Institutions*. New York: The Free Press. p. 106.

25 Anderson, J. (2006) 'Well suited partners: Psychoanalytic research and grounded theory'. *Journal of Child Psychotherapy*. 32 (3): 329-348. p. 76.

26 Canham, H. (2003) 'The relevance of the Oedipus myth to fostered and adopted children'. *Journal of Child Psychotherapy*. 29 (1): 5-19.